GENESIS 1–11

Creation, Sin, and the Nature of God

John MacArthur

THOMAS NELSON
Since 1798

MacArthur Bible Studies

Genesis 1–11: Creation, Sin, and the Nature of God

Published in Nashville, Tennessee, by Nelson Books, an imprint of Thomas Nelson. Nelson Books and Thomas Nelson are registered trademarks of HarperCollins Christian Publishing, Inc.

Originally published in association with the literary agency of Wolgemuth & Associates, Inc. Original layout, design, and writing assistance by Gregory C. Benoit Publishing, Old Mystic, CT.

"Unleashing God's Truth, One Verse at a Time'" is a trademark of Grace to You. All rights reserved.

Thomas Nelson, Inc. titles may be purchased in bulk for educational, business, fundraising, or sales promotional use. For information, please e-mail SpecialMarkets@thomasnelson.com.

Some material from the Introduction, "Keys to the Text," and "Exploring the Meaning" sections are taken from *The MacArthur Bible Commentary*, John MacArthur, copyright © 2005 Thomas Nelson Publishers.

ISBN 978-0-7180-3374-3

First Printing December 2015 / Printed in the United States of America
HB 01.23.2024

CONTENTS

INTRODUCTION

Every story, like every life, has a beginning. It is no surprise, then, to discover that the Bible begins the story of mankind at the very beginning, before there was life of any kind, and planet earth itself had just been shaped. Yet even then there was one life—that of God Himself, who is Life.

As we go through the twelve studies in this book, we will discover that the Bible is not so much the history of mankind as the history of Life—that is, God—and His love and grace toward mankind. The Bible is, in fact, the history of the Messiah: God's Son, Jesus Christ, through whom God shows His grace. God's love and grace toward His creation have always been at work to reveal the Messiah as our Redeemer. But to understand God's plan of redemption, we must first understand that we need a Redeemer. That is what the early chapters of Genesis are all about.

In the twelve lessons that follow, we will examine the origins of the human race and discover exactly where suffering and death originated. We will also learn, among other things, how mankind came to be divided into different races and nationalities, why the world contains such a diversity of cultures and languages, and who committed the first murder. Through it all, we will learn a precious truth about the God who created all things—His love has been involved in human history from the very beginning! He is still involved in it today.

TITLE

The English title "Genesis" comes from the Septuagint (the Greek translation of the Bible) meaning "origins." Genesis serves to introduce the Pentateuch (the first five books of the Old Testament) and the entire Bible. The influence of Genesis in Scripture is demonstrated by the fact that it is quoted more than 35 times in the New Testament, with hundreds of allusions appearing in both Testaments. The story line of salvation, which begins in Genesis 3, is not completed until Revelation 21–22, where the eternal kingdom of redeemed believers is gloriously pictured.

AUTHOR AND DATE

While (1) the author does not identify himself in Genesis, and (2) Genesis ends almost three centuries before Moses was born, both the Old Testament and the New Testament ascribe this composition to Moses (see, e.g., Exodus 17:14; Numbers 33:2; Ezra 6:18; Nehemiah 13:1; Matthew 8:4; Mark 12:26; Luke 16:29; John 5:46). Moses is the fitting author in light of his educational background (see Acts 7:22), and no compelling reasons have been forthcoming to challenge his authorship. Genesis was written after the Exodus (c. 1445 BC) but before Moses' death (c. 1405 BC).

BACKGROUND AND SETTING

The initial setting for Genesis is eternity past. God, by willful act and divine Word, spoke all creation into existence, furnished it, and breathed life into a lump of dirt that He fashioned in His image to become Adam. God made mankind the crowning point of His creation; i.e., His companions who would enjoy fellowship with Him and bring glory to His name.

The historical background for the early events in Genesis is clearly Mesopotamian. While it is difficult to pinpoint precisely the historical moment for which this book was written, Israel first heard Genesis sometime prior to crossing the Jordan River and entering the Promised Land (c. 1405 BC).

Genesis has three distinct sequential geographical settings: (1) Mesopotamia (chapters 1–11); (2) the Promised Land (chapters 12–36); and (3) Egypt (chapters 37–50). The time frames of these three segments are: (1) creation to c. 2090 BC; (2) 2090–1897 BC; and (3) 1897–1804 BC. Genesis covers more time than the remaining books of the Bible combined.

HISTORICAL AND THEOLOGICAL THEMES

In this book of beginnings, God revealed Himself and a worldview to Israel that contrasted, at times sharply, with the worldview of Israel's neighbors. The author made no attempt to defend the existence of God or to present a systematic discussion of His person and works. Rather, Israel's God distinguished Himself clearly from the alleged gods of her neighbors. Theological foundations are revealed, which include God the Father, God the Son, God the Holy Spirit, man, sin, redemption, covenant, promise, Satan and angels, kingdom, revelation, Israel, judgment, and blessing.

Genesis 1–11 (primeval history) reveals the origins of the universe (the beginnings of time and space) and many of the firsts in human experience, such as marriage, family, the Fall, sin, redemption, judgment, and nations. Genesis 12–50 (patriarchal history) explained to Israel how they came into existence as a family whose ancestry could be traced to Eber (hence the "Hebrews"; see Genesis 10:24–25) and even more remotely to Shem, the son of Noah (hence the "Semites"; see Genesis 10:21). God's people came to understand not only their ancestry and family history but also the origins of their institutions, customs, languages, and different cultures, especially basic human experiences such as sin and death.

Because they were preparing to enter Canaan and dispossess the Canaanite inhabitants of their homes and properties, God revealed their enemies' background. In addition, they needed to understand the actual basis of the war they were about to declare in light of the immorality of killing, consistent with the other four books that Moses was writing (Exodus, Leviticus, Numbers, and Deuteronomy). Ultimately, the Jewish nation would understand a selected portion of preceding world history and the inaugural background of Israel as a basis by which they would live in their new beginnings under Joshua's leadership in the land that had previously been promised to Abraham, their original patriarchal forefather.

Genesis 12:1–3 established a primary focus on God's promises to Abraham. This narrowed their view from the entire world of peoples in Genesis 1–11 to one small nation, Israel, through whom God would progressively accomplish His redemptive plan. This underscored Israel's mission to be "a light for the

Gentiles" (Isaiah 42:6). God promised land, descendants (seed), and blessing. This threefold promise became, in turn, the basis of the covenant with Abraham (see Genesis 15:1–20). The rest of Scripture bears out the fulfillment of these promises.

On a larger scale, Genesis 1–11 sets forth a singular message about the character and works of God. In the sequence of accounts which make up these chapters of Scripture, a pattern emerges that reveals God's abundant grace as He responded to the willful disobedience of mankind. Without exception, in each account God increased the manifestation of His grace. But also without exception, man responded in greater sinful rebellion. In biblical words, the more sin abounded the more did God's grace abound (see Romans 5:20).

One final theme of both theological and historical significance that sets Genesis apart from other books of Scripture is that this first book of Scripture corresponds closely with the final book. In the book of Revelation, the paradise that was lost in Genesis will be regained. The apostle John clearly presented the events recorded in his book as future resolutions to the problems that began as a result of the curse in Genesis 3. His focus is on the effects of the Fall in the undoing of creation and the manner in which God rids His creation of the curse effect. In John's own words, "No longer will there be any curse" (Revelation 22:3). Not surprisingly, in the final chapter of God's Word, believers will find themselves back in the garden of Eden, the eternal paradise of God, eating from the tree of life (see Revelation 22:1–14). At that time they will partake, wearing robes washed in the blood of the Lamb (see 22:14).

INTERPRETIVE CHALLENGES

Grasping the individual messages of Genesis that make up the larger plan and purpose of the book presents no small challenge, because both the individual accounts and the book's overall message offer important lessons to faith and works. Genesis presents creation by divine fiat, *ex nihilo*; i.e., "out of nothing." Three traumatic events of epic proportions—namely the Fall, the universal flood, and the dispersion of nations—are presented as historical backdrop in order to understand world history. From Abraham on, the pattern is to focus on God's redemption and blessing.

The customs of Genesis often differ considerably from those of our modern day. They must be explained against their ancient Near Eastern background. Each custom must also be treated according to the immediate context of the passage before any attempt is made to explain it based on customs recorded in extrabiblical sources or even elsewhere in Scripture.

THE WORLD BEFORE ABRAHAM

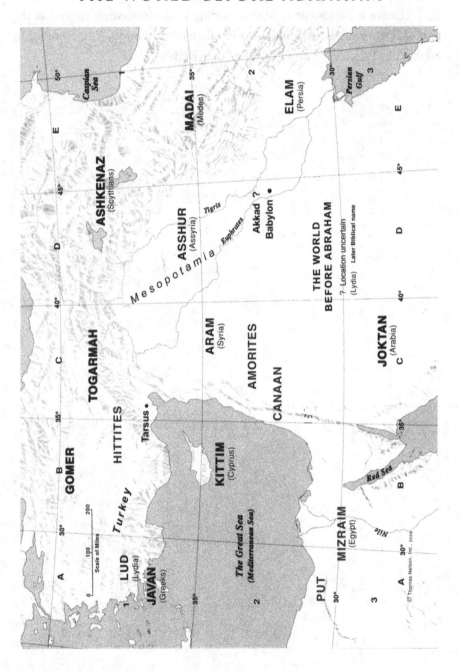

CREATION OF THE WORLD

Genesis 1:1–2:2

DRAWING NEAR

The first chapter of Genesis tells of the creation of the universe. How is that similar or different to what is commonly taught today in public schools?

_____

_____

_____

_____

THE CONTEXT

There is actually no historical background for our opening passage, because there was no history prior to Genesis 1:1. The Bible begins at the very beginning, appropriately enough—and only God is there.

In this chapter, we will meet God, and He will reveal Himself to our eyes right from the beginning of time. We will see Him issuing commands from heaven while also hovering over the waters of the newly forming planet earth.

As we begin our study of God's earliest dealings with mankind, it is important that we properly understand Genesis, the "book of beginnings." Genesis is written as a book of history. It is a literal account of literal people who experienced literal events. It is not a collection of myths, nor is it a figurative treatment of metaphors or abstract concepts. It is not even a "polemic," a book whose sole purpose is to argue against some other teaching or popular belief.

The book of Genesis is intended to teach God's people about His interaction with mankind, beginning at the dawn of creation and continuing through the life of Joseph. In an age when most of the world has embraced the teachings of evolution, God's people may need to recognize that this teaching on the origins of mankind will require an act of faith. However, whether we believe in the teachings of Darwin or the teachings of Moses, we will alike be exercising faith.

Genesis begins not only with an account of the origins of mankind but also all forms of life on earth and even of earth itself. It is not a metaphorical treatment of evolutionary beginnings; it is a literal account of six literal days that God Himself spent creating all that we know as our universe.

[**NOTE:** Refer to the map in the Introduction for information throughout this study.]

KEYS TO THE TEXT

Read Genesis 1:1–2:2, noting the key words and phrases indicated below.

> DAY 1: *God creates planet earth, followed by light. He then separates light from darkness and gives names to both.*

1:1. BEGINNING: The Bible opens, in its very first verse, at the beginning of our physical universe. This does not include heaven, the abode of God, but it does include everything in our plane of creation—stars, sun, planets, and whatever lies beyond that man has not yet discovered.

2. WITHOUT FORM, AND VOID: This Hebrew phrase simply means that the created sphere that we call earth was initially empty and unshaped. Some attempt to find "waste" or "chaos" in this phrase, but one cannot have "chaos" in an empty vessel—which is the essential meaning here. The earth was like an unshaped lump of clay, awaiting the Potter's loving hands.

SPIRIT OF GOD: This is our first glimpse of God's triune nature, existing in three distinct Persons: Father, Son, and Holy Spirit. The Son had not yet taken on human flesh, of course, but we know from John 1 that He was present at creation—indeed, that He was the very agent of creation.

HOVERING: This Hebrew word implies a gentle fluttering and is used to describe a mother hen as she flutters above her chicks. From the very beginning, we see the Spirit of God as He shapes His creation.

3. GOD SAID: God created by His word alone, with the sole exception of mankind. For the rest of creation, He merely spoke His will and it became reality—instantly. The Gospel of John tells us that "all things were made through Him, and without Him nothing was made that was made" (1:3). John refers to Jesus as the Word, and in Genesis 1 we are seeing Him at work.

LIGHT: Some people have argued that there could not have been "light" prior to the sun's creation, but that clearly makes no sense. The sun is not the only source of light in creation. God Himself is light (see 1 John 1:5), and it is entirely possible that the Spirit of God had at this point revealed the Light to God's developing world.

4. GOD DIVIDED THE LIGHT FROM THE DARKNESS: Right from the beginning of creation, God set darkness apart from light. This may seem self-evident in the physical realm, but it will become of deep spiritual significance after Adam sins. This is the first of several divisions that God established at creation.

5. GOD CALLED THE LIGHT DAY: God chose to name some aspects of creation, while giving Adam the authority to name others. In ancient cultures, it was a sign of authority to bestow a name on a person or thing. Thus, God retains to Himself the final authority over the physical elements of His creation, including the cycles of earth that we know as "night" and "day."

THE EVENING AND THE MORNING: Some people also argue that there could not have been an "evening" and a "morning" prior to the creation of the sun, yet it is not the sun that determines the cycles of time—it is the earth's rotation. The planet was revolving on its axis on day 1, and Moses was letting us know that the first day—twenty-four hours—had passed.

FIRST DAY: A popular doctrine (known as the "day/age theory") suggests that the "days" of Genesis 1 actually represent great periods of time—that the "first day" was actually thousands or millions of years long. There are many reasons why this cannot be so, which we will see as we proceed, but the most basic reason is that the book of Genesis is clearly meant to be a historical account of actual people and events. Moses was not writing metaphorically here; he was writing literally. When he said "the evening and the morning were the first day," he meant a literal twenty-four-hour period of time.

DAY 2: *God creates the sky and divides the waters above from the waters on earth.*

6. FIRMAMENT: The sky.

8. GOD CALLED THE FIRMAMENT HEAVEN: Once again, we see God naming the physical aspects of creation, indicating that He is the One in final authority over what we call "the heavens and the earth." He retains authority over mankind's physical environment, including the atmosphere, the planet, and the waters of the sea (see verse 10). This is an important doctrine in the face of modern fears concerning the future inhabitability of our planet.

DAY 3: *God separates dry land from the seas and then creates plant life.*

11. LET THE EARTH BRING FORTH GRASS: The planet is now ready to sustain life, so on day 3 God calls life into existence. This is not sentient life, or creatures that are capable of thought and independent action; that will come on day 5. It is important, from God's perspective, that the environment be fully ready to sustain sentient life prior to the creation of animals, birds, and fish. There must be seas and dry land for the creatures to live in, as well as plants to provide them with food.

ACCORDING TO ITS KIND: Moses reiterated this phrase repeatedly throughout the creation account. This phrase alone precludes any element of evolution being read into Genesis 1, as the chapter states emphatically that grass can only bring forth grass—it cannot evolve into some other life form.

DAY 4: *God creates the stars, sun, moon, and other planets.*

14. LIGHTS IN THE FIRMAMENT: Everything that God made—from plants to animals to heavenly bodies—was complete and fully functioning when created.

LET THEM BE FOR SIGNS AND SEASONS, AND FOR DAYS AND YEARS: God intended from the beginning that mankind would use the stars to gauge the passage of time. They would also serve as signs of His great power. Interestingly, thousands of years later, God would even use a "star" or "great light" to lead the wise men to worship His newborn Son (see Matthew 2:1–12).

16. TWO GREAT LIGHTS: The sun and moon. Here we discover another reason that the "days" of Genesis 1 must be understood as literal, twenty-four-hour time periods. God created plant life on day 3, but the sun does not appear until day 4. Plants could easily survive for twenty-four hours without sunlight, but not for millions of years.

DAY 5: God creates fish and birds.

20. LET THE WATERS ABOUND: On day 5, God created fish and birds. Evolution teaches that birds evolved *from* fish, but Genesis teaches that fish and birds appeared on earth at the same time.

21. ACCORDING TO ITS KIND: Once again, Moses reiterated that fish can only bring forth fish, and birds can only bring forth birds. There is no room in Genesis for the doctrines of evolution.

22. GOD BLESSED THEM: This is the first time that God spoke directly to His creatures. It is significant that His first words were those of blessing.

BE FRUITFUL AND MULTIPLY: This was God's first commandment. There is no negative connotation here—only the positive word of *blessing*. As we will see soon enough, mankind is the only part of God's earthly creation to which He gave the choice of obedience.

DAY 6: God creates land animals, and then finally mankind— directly, by His own hands.

25. GOD SAW THAT IT WAS GOOD: Moses repeated this phrase at each stage of creation. It is God's statement that His creation is good, but it is more than that: it is God's declaration of "it is finished" on each aspect of creation. He created fish and "saw that it was good." He created birds and "saw that it was good." He created land animals and "saw that it was good." In other words, He stated emphatically that the living creatures were created complete, with

5

nothing further to be done. There was no need for those creatures to evolve into something more.

26. LET US MAKE MAN IN OUR IMAGE: This is the first time that God speaks to Himself, and it is significant that He uses the plural "Us." We have already seen God's Spirit hovering over the waters while God speaks His creation into existence. Some have suggested that God is speaking in this verse to the angels, but this cannot be: mankind is created in God's image, not the image of God and the angels. God is revealing His triune nature to creation right from the beginning of time.

ACCORDING TO OUR LIKENESS: Mankind is different from the rest of creation. The earth brought forth each living creature "according to its kind," and all those creatures were made according to the likeness of earth. But God Himself created mankind with His own hands, and man was created according to *God's* likeness. No other part of creation was made in His image.

DOMINION: We have already seen that God retained some aspects of creation under His own authority, but we now discover that He placed other aspects under man's authority—specifically, all sentient life forms.

28. BE FRUITFUL AND MULTIPLY: God is not worried about the overpopulation of the earth. Indeed, the Scriptures often reiterate that children are a blessing from God—the more children, the greater the blessing.

31. IT WAS VERY GOOD: Every element of creation had been "good," which indicates that each life form was complete in itself. Yet the whole of creation was not completed until God had created an overseer to rule over the lower life forms. For this role, He created a very special creature, made in His own image. With the creation of mankind, both male and female, God pronounced that His creation was *more* than good—it was *very* good. This is a doubly emphasized statement that creation was complete and there was nothing further to "evolve."

DAY 7: God declares His work finished and rests.

2:1. FINISHED: Moses reiterated, yet again, that all of creation was completed in six days. There is nothing ongoing, nothing left incomplete, and nothing that is evolving any further. Modern science teaches us that evolution is still continuing—that the work of creation is never complete—but this is directly contrary to the teachings of Genesis.

2. GOD ENDED HIS WORK ... AND HE RESTED: With the dawn of the seventh day, God ended His work and "rested" from creating. He certainly did not rest due to weariness—He simply abstained from further creative work and, in doing so, established the pattern for man's work cycle. Later, the Sabbath ordinance of Moses would be based in the creation week (see Exodus 20:8–11). The Sabbath would be God's sacred, ordained day in the weekly cycle.

UNLEASHING THE TEXT

1) What aspects of creation do you find interesting or surprising?

_____

_____

_____

_____

_____

2) In what ways is mankind different from the rest of creation? In what ways is it similar?

_____

_____

_____

_____

_____

_____

3) What details of creation disagree with the doctrines of evolution? Can the two views—creation by God versus evolution—be reconciled in any way?

_____

_____

_____

_____

4) What hints do you find that show the love of God in Genesis 1:1–2:2?

_____

_____

_____

_____

_____

EXPLORING THE MEANING

God loves His creation. One of the most striking things that we discover in Genesis 1 is God's love toward all creation. This becomes a vital theme throughout Scripture, culminating in the costly sacrifice that God's own Son would make for mankind on the cross.

We find God's Spirit hovering above the waters of creation before the earth was even shaped, and His presence is similar to that of a mother hen guarding her chicks. God spoke to His creatures as they were created, and His words were all blessing and encouragement: "Be fruitful! Multiply! Be blessed!"

God the Creator also concluded each day by stepping back and assessing His own work—and each day He declared that it was good. Clearly, God was pleased by the work of His hands and loved His entire creation.

There is order in God's creation. There was nothing haphazard in God's creative work. He deliberately separated things that should be kept separate, such as light and darkness, dry land and the oceans. He created environments that were specifically designed to support different forms of life, such as the seas for fish and the sky for birds.

God also named certain elements of creation, such as the elements of our environment. The notion of bestowing a name on something indicates authority and lordship, and God has retained to Himself the lordship over His created environment. On the other hand, He gave mankind lordship over the lower orders of life, including fish, birds, land animals, and "every creeping thing that creeps on the earth" (Genesis 1:26).

This order within creation has wide-ranging implications throughout Scripture. For instance, God promised mankind after the Flood that the earth's environment would always sustain life (see Genesis 8:22). He reiterated man's authority over the animal kingdom (see 9:2–3) while also reiterating the sanctity of human life (see 9:5–6). Paul referred back to Genesis when he addressed issues of order within the church (e.g., see 1 Corinthians 11).

Mankind is unique in all of creation. Genesis underscores repeatedly that mankind is different from the rest of creation. God spoke a command and fish appeared, birds appeared, and plants and animals burst forth from the earth—but mankind was created differently. We share the same original material with the rest of creation, as God used the dust of the earth to create us (see Genesis 2:7). However, the Lord did more than merely speak a command when He created Adam: He fashioned the dust with His own hands and breathed life directly into his nostrils.

Only human beings are created in the image of God. This in itself is a deep subject for consideration. What does it mean to be created in God's image? In an intellectual sense, Adam and Eve were like God in that they could exercise reason and understanding. In a moral sense, they were like God because they were good and sinless. (That, of course, would change when they sinned.)

Again, there is no room in Genesis for the notions of evolution. We gain nothing by suggesting that the six days of creation were actually millions of years, because Genesis 1 makes it clear that God did not use evolution to create mankind—or any other aspect of the world that He made.

REFLECTING ON THE TEXT

5) How does this passage in Genesis 1:1–2:2 emphasize the gentleness and love of God toward creation? What does this suggest about His view of you personally?

_____

_____

_____

_____

_____

6) What aspects of creation did God name? What aspects did He allow mankind to name? What are the implications of this?

_____

_____

_____

_____

7) Why did God "rest" on the seventh day? What does it mean that He blessed the seventh day?

_____

_____

_____

_____

8) How do you respond to the fact that Genesis 1 disagrees with the teachings of modern science?

_____

_____

_____

_____

PERSONAL RESPONSE

9) How do you respond to the concept of God's created order? How do you respond to the idea that God has ordained levels of authority?

_____

_____

_____

_____

10) What do you learn about God's love from these passages in Genesis 1:1–2:2? How does this affect your relationship with Him?

_____

_____

_____

_____

_____

2

ADAM AND EVE
Genesis 2:3–25

DRAWING NEAR

The Bible tells us that God put Adam "in the garden of Eden to tend and keep it" (Genesis 2:15) and that He created Eve to be "a helper comparable" to Adam (verse 18). What do those two verses bring to mind about the roles of men and women?

_____

_____

_____

_____

THE CONTEXT

In Genesis 1, we learned that God made mankind, both male and female, on day 6 of the creation week. When God created man, He did a number of things that were different from His creation of all other life forms on earth. First, He picked up some soil in His hands and fashioned man, just as a sculptor might mold clay. He breathed life directly into man's nostrils. He created mankind in two stages, first the male and then the female *from the male*. None of these things were done for any other creature in all of creation.

13

But God wasn't finished once He created man. As we take a closer look at day 6, we discover that God created a special garden just for the man and his wife. This was a separate place within creation, not a special act of creation. God planted a garden using the plants and life forms He had already created that week, and He created this garden specifically for the pleasure of His highest creature.

Finally, day 6 saw the newly created man getting started on the work for which he had been created in the first place: taking charge of the rest of God's creation. God brought His newly fashioned animals—just a day or two old—and paraded them before the man to see what he would name them. Adam spent his first day of life getting to know God's creation and bestowing names on all the animals. Then he underwent surgery, awoke to discover a newly created woman, and got married!

It was a very busy day.

KEYS TO THE TEXT

Read Genesis 2:3–25, noting the key words and phrases indicated below.

> CREATING MAN: *God rolls up His sleeves and creates a special being that bears His own image.*

2:7. GOD FORMED MAN: The first thing that strikes us about man's creation is the fact that God got His hands dirty in the process. All other aspects of creation—from the advent of light through the higher forms of animals—were created by *divine fiat*, by God's verbal command: "Let there be . . . and there was." But with mankind, God formed Adam as if with His own hands. The reference to hands, of course, is metaphorical since God is a spirit and does not have a physical body. Yet the language indicates a greater level of intimate involvement in the creation of man than in God's other creative acts.

OF THE DUST OF THE GROUND: Here alone is the one and only element that mankind shares in common with the rest of creation: we were created from the dust of the ground, just as were the animals and plants. That is to say, God used the same initial material—dirt—to create mankind and the animals. But He did *not* use the animals themselves as the basic material for mankind or evolve humans out of the lower orders. Man shares the basic physical elements with the rest of creation, but our origins are very different than modern evolutionary theory proposes.

BREATH OF LIFE: Adam came to life when God breathed His life into the inanimate clay. This is the foundation of what it means to be created in God's image: we are both physical and spiritual beings. The spirit of man bears the resemblance of God Himself, even as our physical beings bear a resemblance to other physical life forms in this world.

PLANTING A GARDEN: After creating man, God gets His hands dirty again (metaphorically speaking), this time planting a special place for man to live and work.

8. GOD PLANTED A GARDEN: This is not some special, secondary act of creation, as some have supposed. God planted a special garden so that His greatest creation—man—might have a special place to live and work. This is another demonstration of God's great loving-kindness toward His creation. The world as it existed already would have been a habitable paradise for Adam and Eve, yet God went above and beyond to create a special paradise within a paradise for His favored creature.

9. PLEASANT TO THE SIGHT AND GOOD FOR FOOD: This is another remarkable demonstration of the generous and tender love of God for His creation. It would have been enough that He provided His creatures with a safe place to live and plenty of food and water to sustain their lives, but He went beyond this and made everything a pleasure. God's creatures must eat in order to survive, but it is also enjoyable. Plants and trees provide man's needed food for survival, and they are also lovely to look at. Evolution, of course, cannot explain this element of creation, but the Bible makes it clear that all beauty and pleasure flow from the character of the Creator.

TREE OF LIFE: This appears to have been a unique tree, one of a kind, that God had planted near the center of Eden. Adam must have observed it and perhaps even eaten of its fruit (see Genesis 2:16), thus sustaining his life. When he failed, all mankind lost all access to the tree; however, it will become available once again in the New Jerusalem—where it will grow in abundance (see Revelation 22).

15

TREE OF THE KNOWLEDGE OF GOOD AND EVIL: Like the tree of life, this tree did not possess any magical properties capable of bestowing knowledge on Adam. It served merely in a symbolic capacity to provide Adam with a tangible test of obedience. Adam already had the knowledge of good, because he knew God; however, by eating the forbidden fruit, he would gain a deadly and irreversible knowledge of evil—by experiencing it firsthand.

15. TO TEND IT AND KEEP IT: God intended that mankind should work, even before sin and death entered the world. It is part of being made in God's image: mankind has a specific job to do, unlike the rest of creation. Before the Fall, however, man's work brought genuine pleasure and satisfaction. It was Adam's sin that introduced the elements of drudgery and frustration into work (see Genesis 3:17–19).

THE FIRST NEGATIVE: God introduces a new element into creation: a commandment with a negative result. For the first time, God allows one of His creatures the option of disobedience.

16. YOU MAY FREELY EAT: God's original creation included an abundance of freedom, pleasure, and satisfaction. In fact, nothing whatsoever was off limits or forbidden (with one small exception), and man was free to do whatever he pleased.

17. BUT: It is significant that God issued this stipulation—the first negative command in all of creation—to man. God told no other creature to refrain from anything. This is yet another element of being created in God's image: the capacity to understand right from wrong and to make moral decisions. Note that Eve had not yet been created—the responsibility for obeying or disobeying this commandment fell on the shoulders of Adam alone, not Adam and Eve together.

YOU SHALL NOT EAT: It was such a small stipulation! "Eat from every tree in the garden; eat to your heart's content! Enjoy every aspect of My creation, with nothing forbidden except this one small thing: don't eat from this one tree." Obedience to God could not have been any easier. However, right from the beginning, mankind could not obey even this one small command of God.

IN THE DAY THAT YOU EAT OF IT YOU SHALL SURELY DIE: This statement contains two important elements: (1) death did not exist in the world prior to Adam's sin, and (2) the curse of death involves more than the physical death of the body. God created all things perfectly, and He did not intend for any of His creatures to die, suffer, or be in poverty, sickness, or danger of any kind. However, God made it clear from the outset that if Adam were to disobey, he would incur the necessary penalty for his act of rebellion—and that penalty would be death. Adam did not drop dead on the day that he ate of the fruit, but his relationship with God was immediately cut off, which indicates that the death of sin was both physical and spiritual. Moreover, physical death became an immediate reality in creation—beginning with the animal that God killed to properly clothe Adam and Eve. The fact that death did not exist in the world prior to Adam's sin further proves that God did not use evolution to create mankind, since evolution requires that death (natural selection) exist if evolution is to occur.

> *NOT GOOD: Another first occurs here: an element of creation that God declares "not good."*

18. IT IS NOT GOOD: This statement is almost jarring because it is so different from all of God's other statements during the creation week. He had repeatedly pronounced that His creation was good, yet here He suddenly states that something is *not* good. This underscores the fact that God's creation of mankind was incomplete.

HELPER COMPARABLE TO HIM: Part of Adam's calling was to "be fruitful and multiply" (Genesis 1:28), which he obviously could not do alone. He was responsible as the caretaker over the rest of creation, an authority that was his alone (see verse 19); nonetheless, he was made complete only when complemented by the woman. This concept of "helper" suggests that the woman holds full equality before God as co-image bearer, while also being subject to the headship of Adam.

19. BROUGHT THEM TO ADAM: God brought the animals to Adam, which again demonstrates his dominion over all creatures. This is comparable to the angelic host who presented themselves before God (see Job 1); it is a sign of submission to authority.

THAT WAS ITS NAME: As part of Adam's authority over the lower orders, whatever name he bestowed on a creature became its name. This responsibility of bestowing a name was not undertaken lightly, because in ancient times a person's name was considered a thing of power—it defined or encapsulated the very nature of the one being named. Therefore, Adam needed to know and understand the creatures that he was naming, not merely assign them some random verbal sounds. We still see this naming convention today, as we have birds called woodpeckers and sapsuckers and so forth. The fact that Adam could comprehend the natures of so many creatures in just one day suggests that he was indeed a perfect man—intelligent and wise and creative to a remarkable degree.

> CREATING WOMAN: *Adam is given the chance to find himself a mate. Naturally, that is a failure, so God creates a helper perfectly suitable for him.*

20. THERE WAS NOT FOUND A HELPER COMPARABLE TO HIM: It is interesting that God declared it "not good" for Adam to be without a helper and then postponed creating Eve until after Adam had named the animals. A likely reason for this is that it gave Adam the opportunity to discover for himself that he had no equal in creation. The appearance of Eve would then be all the more delightful.

21. ONE OF HIS RIBS: The rib cage is vital for human life. It protects the internal organs from damage, enables a person to inhale and exhale, and provides basic body structure. These analogies can help us understand the woman's role as "helper," as she helps to refresh and encourage her husband, seeks his protection and well-being, and brings him strength and support.

22. HE BROUGHT HER TO THE MAN: God did not have Adam and Eve meet together in the garden; instead, He brought her before the man. This is similar to the way in which He brought the animals before Adam for naming. Once again, it suggests that Adam had a degree of headship over Eve.

23. SHE SHALL BE CALLED WOMAN: Adam bestowed a name on his wife, which again demonstrates his headship over her. It also demonstrated that he understood her nature and character because, as we have discussed the one giving the name had to understand the nature of the one he was naming. Beyond these elements, however, was the fact that he was responsible for her welfare—a concept that Paul carried out further in Ephesians 5:22–33.

24. THEY SHALL BECOME ONE FLESH: God intended permanent, monogamous marriage for mankind from the beginning of creation. Divorce, unfaithfulness, polygamy—to say nothing of modern notions of homosexual "marriage"—are all inventions of sinful man that go against God's original design.

GOING DEEPER

In Romans 5:12–19, Paul explains some of the implications of Adam and Eve's sin. Read that passage and note the key words and phrases below.

> FIRST ADAM AND LAST ADAM: *Adam brought sin and death into the world, but he was just "a type of Him who was to come." His failure provides a vivid contrast to Christ, the Last Adam.*

5:12. THROUGH ONE MAN: This refers to Adam. It was Adam's disobedience, not Eve's, that brought sin into the world. The sin nature was transmitted through Adam, and all of Adam's descendants became sinners by nature. This is a law of creation, for God declared that "like brings forth like," that a cow can only produce a cow, and a sinner can only reproduce a sinner.

DEATH THROUGH SIN: Death did not exist in the world prior to Adam's failure. It was his sin, and that alone, which subjected all creation to the curse of death.

14. WHO IS A TYPE OF HIM WHO WAS TO COME: Jesus is called "the Last Adam" in the New Testament (e.g., 1 Corinthians 15:45). It is through Him, and Him alone, that mankind can find release from the curse of death. We "die" to the "old Adam" and are "born again" to the Last Adam when we accept the salvation provided by Jesus Christ.

UNLEASHING THE TEXT

1) When have you seen God's generous provision in your own life—for basic needs as well as pleasure and joy?

_____

_____

_____

_____

_____

2) Why did God create Adam and Eve in a special way?

_____

_____

_____

_____

_____

3) What do these passages in Genesis 2:3–25 teach about sin and death? What do they teach about forgiveness and eternal life?

_____

_____

_____

_____

_____

4) What roles were given to men? To women? Do these roles still apply today?

_____

_____

_____

_____

_____

_____

Exploring the Meaning

Adam had headship over Eve. This concept is controversial in today's society, which equates authority with despotism. Yet male headship was established at the time of creation, and it plays an important role in the structure of the church and the home even today.

Paul referred back to these important chapters in Genesis when he addressed the roles of men and women. God gave the commandment to Adam, not to Adam and Eve, and He held Adam solely responsible for the actions of his wife when she was deceived by Satan.

It might also be noted that Adam serves as a contrast to Christ. As Adam was the head of sinful humanity, so Christ is the head of redeemed humanity. As Adam's sin brought death to all mankind, so Christ's perfection brought salvation to our race. Whereas the first Adam brought separation from God and a curse, the last Adam (Jesus Christ) offers reconciliation to God and eternal life to all who believe in Him.

Man needs woman. God created Adam first and gave him lordship over creation. But He then permitted Adam to discover for himself that there was no other creature in the world that complemented him. He learned two valuable lessons from this.

First, he learned that he needed help. He was capable of naming the animals by himself, but to fully carry out his job as gardener and caretaker over the animals, he needed another by his side. And he was certainly not going to "be fruitful and multiply" without a mate.

Second, there was no other creature that bore the image of God. Adam got to know all the animals in creation well enough to bestow names on them, and in the process he discovered that no other creature complemented his unique image. He needed someone very special for this purpose. This is an important corollary to the principle of headship, because headship is not the same as "lording over" another person (see Ephesians 5:22–33, where Paul explains that headship is expressed in sacrificial service and loving leadership). Without Eve, Adam was incomplete—and God Himself declared that this was "not good."

Marriage is a sacred bond established by God at the time of creation. God's definition of marriage is one man for one woman. There was never any allowance for sexual relations outside of that bond, nor was there any allowance for divorce or any other types of sexual unions.

It is no accident that the world today is attacking the institution of marriage so viciously. The enemy of mankind—the devil himself—hates God's created order and is working tenaciously to destroy the sacredness of the marriage bond. His goal today is the same as it was in the garden of Eden: to turn God's order upside down.

REFLECTING ON THE TEXT

5) Why is marriage so important in the world today? What happens when the family structure that God ordained is disrupted?

_____

_____

_____

_____

_____

6) In practical terms, what does "headship" mean in the family? In the church? In other areas of society?

_____

_____

_____

_____

7) Why did God use one of Adam's ribs to create Eve? What does this suggest about the roles that men and women have today?

_____

_____

_____

_____

8) In what ways does Christ perfectly fulfill the roles for which Adam was created?

_____

_____

_____

_____

PERSONAL RESPONSE

9) What responsibilities has God given to you? For what people might you be accountable? How well are you fulfilling those responsibilities?

_____

_____

_____

_____

10) Who has headship over you in your life? How much of God's headship do you submit to in your relationship with Him?

_____

_____

_____

_____

3

THE FALL OF MAN
Genesis 3:1–24

DRAWING NEAR

When Eve spoke with Satan in the garden of Eden, she both added and subtracted from God's words, with disastrous results. How do you see people attempting to add or subtract from God's Word today? What are the results?

_____

_____

_____

_____

THE CONTEXT

God has just finished creating the entire universe, culminating with His highest creation on day 6: mankind. We do not know the exact amount of time between the first Sabbath day, when God rested from creating, and the day when Adam ruined it all by committing sin. It would seem, however, that it was not long. For all we know, it may have been that very first Sabbath day!

God had specifically told Adam—and Adam alone—that he could eat from any tree in the garden except the tree of knowledge of good and evil. Of course, we cannot say with certainty that God did not reiterate the commandment later in Eve's presence, but the Scriptures seem to indicate that Adam was responsible for telling Eve. This touches upon the doctrine of headship, which we examined in the last session.

Also remember that as our passage opens, there is no death in the world. All of God's creation is at perfect peace—lions gambol about in play with lambs, sharks swim together with bait fish. And serpents have legs! (At least, that would appear to be the case from this chapter.) Everything is perfect; there is no conflict, no fear, no sickness, no fighting—no death.

Adam is about to change all that.

Keys to the Text

Read Genesis 3:1–24, noting the key words and phrases indicated below.

> THE TEMPTATION: *We now fast-forward a short time. God has created Eve from Adam's rib, and we see her standing beside the tree of knowledge of good and evil.*

3:1. THE SERPENT: The New Testament tells us clearly that the one speaking to Eve was Satan himself (see 2 Corinthians 11:3; Revelation 12:9). Apparently, he took possession of a serpent and used its body and vocal organs to speak to Eve.

AND HE SAID: Did snakes talk in Eden? We do not know, because Scripture does not tell us. However, we do learn in this chapter that snakes did not slither on their bellies prior to the fall of mankind. They may have even had wings! The ancient myths and traditions of dragons are worldwide—every culture and society knows what a dragon looks like. It is possible that, before Adam's sin, the serpent might have looked like a great, winged dragon.

TO THE WOMAN: It is interesting that Satan approached Eve with his lies rather than Adam. After all, Adam had headship over creation—and to corrupt him would be to corrupt all creation. This, of course, was Satan's very design, but he chose to corrupt Adam by first overturning the created order. He wanted to remove Adam from headship altogether and replace him with Eve.

HAS GOD INDEED SAID: The first thing the evil one did in his seduction of the woman was to question the word of God. Remember that Eve was not present when God gave the commandment, so she was relying on what Adam had told her. Thus, Satan was tempting Eve to doubt both God's word and her husband's reliability.

YOU SHALL NOT EAT OF EVERY TREE: Satan now tried to get Eve to doubt the reliability of God's word by deliberately misquoting God. This two-step process planted the seeds in Eve's mind that God is a stingy ogre who denied His creatures the very things that they need and crave. This is exactly the opposite of God's true nature.

> THE MISTAKE: *Eve makes her first mistake by debating with the devil. The devil is not interested in learning the truth, as his goal is only to confuse and mislead.*

2. WE MAY EAT THE FRUIT OF THE TREES: Eve subtly misquoted God herself at this point. God's actual words were, "Of *every* tree of the garden you may *freely* eat" (Genesis 2:16, italics added). God's words imply immense generosity and freedom—a sense that is lost in Eve's words. It is a subtle distinction, but it is always best to quote God's words exactly.

3. NOR SHALL YOU TOUCH IT: Here Eve makes an addition to God's words. It is quite possible that Adam added this stipulation, intending to avoid temptation in the first place by creating his own rules of not even touching the tree. This was the birth of legalism, whereby men add to God's Word with good intentions, hoping to avoid temptation. Yet legalism always fails, just as this stipulation failed. Whatever the reason, in the end Eve corrupted God's words, first by subtracting from them and then by adding to them (see Revelation 22:18–19).

LEST YOU DIE: Here again we find Eve again subtly misquoting God. God said, "You shall surely die," which leaves no doubt whatsoever of the outcome: eat the fruit and die. Eve's wording, on the other hand, leaves some element of doubt: "Eat the fruit, and you might die." Again, quoting God's Word exactly is important.

> THE LIE: *Satan now speaks his native language. Every word from his mouth is a lie or tainted by a lie.*

4. YOU WILL NOT SURELY DIE: Satan's first words were insidious suggestions to mislead and cause doubt in Eve's mind. But now he tells an outright

lie—the first in God's brand-new creation. Jesus stated that Satan "was a murderer from the beginning, and does not stand in the truth, because there is no truth in him. When he speaks a lie, he speaks from his own resources, for he is a liar and the father" of lies (John 8:44). The enemy's lies led to death, and thus he "was a murderer from the beginning" of creation.

5. FOR GOD KNOWS: Here is another subtle poison of the devil: he hinted that God was withholding some secret information—some secret "higher knowledge"—in order to keep Eve under domination.

YOUR EYES WILL BE OPENED, AND YOU WILL BE LIKE GOD: This is the invention of an ancient heresy called Gnosticism. The Gnostics were active during the early church, and Paul addressed their heresy in Colossians and elsewhere. Gnosticism teaches that a person needs to acquire some secret "higher knowledge" in order to understand God and His Word. This heresy is alive and thriving in modern society and is found at the root of evolution and false religions such as New Age cults.

THE ORIGINAL SIN: We now have the painful task of watching the father of the human race reject the lordship of God and submit himself—first to his wife, and then ultimately to the devil.

KNOWING GOOD AND EVIL: Adam and Eve already knew good. They discovered that knowing evil was a very bad thing.

6. GOOD FOR FOOD ... PLEASANT TO THE EYES ... MAKE ONE WISE: Eve was tempted by "the lust of the flesh, the lust of the eyes, and the pride of life," as John described (1 John 2:16).

SHE TOOK OF ITS FRUIT AND ATE: Eve was deceived into eating the forbidden fruit (see 2 Corinthians 11:3). The deception began as a small doubt concerning the character of God, grew into doubt of her husband's trustworthiness, flourished into the three areas of worldly lust, and bore the fruit of sinful actions.

HER HUSBAND WITH HER: It is entirely possible that Adam was standing nearby during this entire conversation and temptation. Whether he was or not, God ultimately held him responsible.

AND HE ATE: Adam was not deceived (see 1 Timothy 2:14); he sinned knowingly, deliberately, and willfully. Again, because God had given him headship over the human race, it was his sin—not Eve's—that led to the curse and the sinful nature that have been part of human life ever since.

THE RESULTS: Somehow that piece of fruit didn't taste as good as promised. This is always the case with sin.

7. THE EYES OF BOTH OF THEM WERE OPENED: This suggests that Adam and Eve did, in fact, gain knowledge from their transgression. However, it turned out to be a knowledge of evil, shame, and death.

THEY KNEW THAT THEY WERE NAKED: This is not "self-discovery," as some have suggested. Adam already had self-awareness when he was created (see Genesis 2:20–23). Rather, this was self-obsession: Adam and Eve had turned their attention away from one another and toward themselves. Thus was born the modern "self-esteem" movement.

THEY SEWED FIG LEAVES TOGETHER AND MADE THEMSELVES COVERINGS: Adam and Eve were quite correct that their shame needed to be covered, but they had yet to learn what that covering would cost. Although they could cover their physical bodies, they were unable to cover their guilt. They needed a covering for sin.

THE CONFRONTATION: God comes looking for Adam, but He does so with a quiet calmness, not in wrath. Tragically, sin has already separated man from Him.

8. THE SOUND OF THE LORD GOD: The Hebrew word for "sound" can also mean "voice." Evidently, God came into Eden calling Adam's name. There is a gentleness about this phrase—God is not bellowing out in anger.

WALKING IN THE GARDEN IN THE COOL OF THE DAY: This seems to imply it was a regular habit of the Lord's to come into the garden to speak with Adam, perhaps on a daily basis. Adam had the incomparable privilege of speaking with God Himself, face-to-face, as one man speaks with another. This privilege was about to be lost.

ADAM AND HIS WIFE HID THEMSELVES: The moment Adam sinned, he and his wife were filled with shame. This guilt they had been laden with for the first time prompted them to try to hide themselves from God's presence.

AMONG THE TREES OF THE GARDEN: The absurdity of a person thinking that he can hide himself from God is bad enough, but to think that he can hide behind a tree is ludicrous. Yet this is the exact mindset of the world, as mankind habitually convinces himself that God cannot see his deeds. It is also worth noting that it was a tree that provided Adam with the chance to sin, and now he was hoping that the trees would shield him from the presence of God. This, too, is a principle of the world system: mankind turns to the things of the world for pleasure, satisfaction, and gain but discovers too late that those same things will avail him nothing when he is finally in the presence of his Creator.

9. GOD CALLED TO ADAM: In this small phrase we get our first glimpse of the tremendous grace and patience of God. He came into the garden to look for Adam, calling out to him even as he attempted to hide. Notice also that God was calling to Adam, not to Adam and Eve. He had given Adam responsibility for the welfare of his wife, and God was now calling him to account.

WHERE ARE YOU? This is the first time in Scripture that God asks a question. It is not because God didn't *know* where Adam was, but rather it was God's way of drawing out a confession. It also underscored that something was now very different in their relationship. Adam had never hidden before, and the fact that he was now trying to hide—so that God would ask where he was—was indicative of the guilt and shame that he was feeling.

11. WHO TOLD YOU THAT YOU WERE NAKED? Here we find God asking another question to which He already knew the answer. The Lord was gently trying to lead Adam to confess his sin. The answer to the question was, of course, "nobody." Nobody *needed* to tell Adam that he was naked; it was self-evident, as his innocence had been lost and his conscience awakened to sin.

HAVE YOU EATEN FROM THE TREE? This was yet another question to which God already knew the answer. God was not seeking answers to things that He did not know; rather, He was seeking reconciliation with Adam. However, that reconciliation could only come if Adam first confessed his sin.

SHIFTING THE BLAME: Adam now sets the pattern of mankind for all time—he blames someone else. Yet God gently leads him to a small confession of sin.

12. THE WOMAN: Adam passed the blame rather than confess.

WHOM YOU GAVE TO BE WITH ME: First Adam blamed Eve, and then he went a step further and blamed God! After all, it had to be God's fault that he had sinned, since it was God who had brought Eve into his life. This is a perfect example of the convoluted logic that sinners use to justify themselves. We are all sons of Adam.

AND I ATE: Here, at last, was a limp, halfhearted almost-confession of sin. Yet it was enough, and God in His grace accepted it as a confession.

13. WHAT IS THIS YOU HAVE DONE? God now asked Eve the same question that He had asked of Adam, offering her the same opportunity for confession of sin.

THE SERPENT DECEIVED ME: This was actually quite true, yet it still did not exonerate Eve from her guilt. She was following Adam's example here by passing blame to someone else.

AND I ATE: Still following Adam's example, Eve made a halfhearted confession of her sin. Yet, once again, God in His grace accepted it as a confession of guilt.

THE CURSE: God responds by informing His creation of what will result from Adam's sin. This is not God ranting and cursing; He is telling them what will follow naturally. Indeed, He brings in a promise of His grace.

14. GOD SAID TO THE SERPENT: Notice that God did not ask the serpent any questions. This is an important distinction, as God did not give the devil any opportunity to confess and repent. God's plan of salvation, as provided through the death and resurrection of the sinless Son of God, was available only to the descendants of Adam. He offered no opportunity for salvation to Satan or his demonic minions.

YOU ARE CURSED: This passage is technically not a covenant between God and man, yet it does represent the first such transaction between God and His creatures after the fall of mankind. The curse itself began with Satan and his minions, as they were the ultimate source of mankind's sorrow. The devil has no hope of repentance or reconciliation with God.

14. ON YOUR BELLY YOU SHALL GO: It is popular today to suggest that this was just a figurative curse—that serpents never had legs. However, that is

not the thrust of this passage at all. God was telling Adam, Eve, and the serpent how things were going to *change* because of sin, and those changes would affect every order of creation—including snakes. It is not speculation to conclude that the snake lost its ability to walk or fly on the day that Adam fell. It is fitting that the agent that caused mankind to fall should also land on its belly.

15. HE SHALL BRUISE YOUR HEAD, AND YOU SHALL BRUISE HIS HEEL: The Hebrew word translated " bruise" can also mean "to crush." A bruised or crushed heel is not a deadly wound, but a crushed head is fatal. God was telling mankind that the evil one would one day bruise His Servant, Jesus Christ, but the Son of God would crush the head of the serpent once and for all. In this, we have our first glimpse of God's plan of salvation for mankind—a plan that He revealed on the very day of man's first sin!

16. IN PAIN YOU SHALL BRING FORTH CHILDREN: God's original plan for childbirth and child-rearing had been painless and free of sorrow—pure joy unalloyed with any form of sadness.

YOUR DESIRE SHALL BE FOR YOUR HUSBAND, AND HE SHALL RULE OVER YOU: This same Hebrew phrasing is used in Genesis 4:7, where God told Cain that "sin lies at the door. And its desire is for you, but you should rule over it." God had ordained from the time of creation that man and woman should live together in harmony and cooperation, each perfectly content and satisfied with his or her role. But now sin had corrupted that relationship, and the woman would strive to take control. This was the birth of feminism, which is not a modern invention at all.

17. BECAUSE YOU HAVE HEEDED THE VOICE OF YOUR WIFE: Note that Adam's sin was twofold. First, he "heeded the voice" of his wife; that is, he submitted himself voluntarily to her leadership. Second, he ate the forbidden fruit. Eve fell into sin when she was seduced into rejecting the leadership of her husband. Adam fell into sin when he went along with that foolish plan. In this way, Satan accomplished his initial desire: to turn the created order upside down.

CURSED IS THE GROUND FOR YOUR SAKE: Adam's sin had consequences that reached far beyond himself. His sin brought death and sorrow to all creation, from the human race all the way down to the dust of the ground from which mankind had been created. This was the first time that humans were confronted with the sad fact that one man's sin would bring suffering on many who are innocent. However, this was balanced with the wonderful news that God's Son would bring grace and salvation to many who were *not* innocent.

IN TOIL YOU SHALL EAT OF IT: When God placed Adam in the garden, his work was a source of joy and fulfillment. All of creation cooperated with Adam as the animals paraded themselves before him in a sign of submission to his dominion. Now, all creation would begin to rebel against mankind's headship, even as Adam himself had rebelled against the headship of God—and as Eve had rebelled against the headship of Adam. Note that the curse touched man and woman in the very seat of their respective roles and sources of satisfaction. The woman would bear children with pain, and the man would work the soil with sweat and sorrow.

19. TO DUST YOU SHALL RETURN: Adam and Eve—and all their descendants for all time—were now subject to death. If Adam had not sinned, we would never have to return to the dust from which we were made. Our relationship with God would be perfect, and we would never know suffering or sickness. But now, because of sin, mankind is subject to the curse of death and decay.

THE COVERING: Adam and Eve had made a pathetic attempt to cover their own shame. Now they would discover that their shame can only be covered by God Himself—at a high price.

21. GOD MADE TUNICS OF SKIN, AND CLOTHED THEM: Adam and Eve learned that their shame indeed needed to be covered, but not in the way they had anticipated. First, they could not cover their shame themselves—the covering could only come from God. Second, that covering had to cover them completely—the fig leaves they had sewn were insufficient. (The Hebrew word in verse 7 means "loincloth," but here it refers to a piece of clothing that covered the entire torso.) Third, that covering could only come with the shedding of innocent blood, as God had to take the life of at least one innocent animal to provide the skins. This is clearly a picture of the final cost of salvation provided by God's own Son.

24. HE DROVE OUT THE MAN: This was both an act of judgment and an act of mercy on God's part. The judgment came because God could not tolerate sin in His presence, so man had to leave. The grace, however, was ironically

the assurance that man would die—that he would not live forever under the horrible curse of sin, decay, and death. "It is appointed for men to die once" (Hebrews 9:27), but this death can free us from the curse of death forever through the blood of Jesus Christ.

HE PLACED CHERUBIM: Later in Israel's history, two cherubim or angelic figures guarded the Ark of the Covenant and the Holy of Holies in the tabernacle (see Exodus 25:18–22), where God communed with His people.

UNLEASHING THE TEXT

1) What was the nature of Eve's sin? What led her into it?

_____

_____

_____

_____

_____

_____

2) What was the nature of Adam's sin? What were its results?

_____

_____

_____

_____

_____

_____

3) Why might Eve have added the stipulation not to even touch the forbidden fruit? What did that stipulation accomplish?

_____

_____

_____

_____

4) In what ways have you seen the curse carried out in your own life? Give some real examples.

_____

_____

_____

_____

EXPLORING THE MEANING

Debating with the devil leads to sin. Eve's first mistake was to stand around chatting with a creature whose initial words to her challenged the word of God. God's command to Adam was perfectly clear, but the devil made it a point to make God's word seem confusing, subtle, and unclear.

He uses this same tactic today. Even many who label themselves as Christians make it a point to bring confusion concerning the very clear teachings of Scripture. They claim that the Bible can't possibly mean what it says in plain language, and the subtle undertone of such teachings is that a person needs some higher form of knowledge to fully comprehend the Word of God. This is modern Gnosticism, the same technique the devil used in the garden of Eden.

When someone challenges the clear teachings of Scripture, do not waste time and energy debating it with him or her.

God never tempts us to sin. God placed the tree of knowledge of good and evil within the garden to offer Adam the opportunity to obey voluntarily, not to tempt him to disobey. This may seem like a subtle distinction, but it is an important concept to understand.

As descendants of Adam, it is easy for us to shirk our responsibility when we sin. We speak glibly about "falling into sin" and being "faced with temptation," but this suggests that we are not responsible for our own actions and can hardly be blamed.

When we face temptation, we must recognize that it is an opportunity to demonstrate our determination to obey God. Temptation is merely the desire to disobey God's commands, while obedience visibly demonstrates our love for God.

Sin results in separation. Adam's sin separated him from God. He had enjoyed daily communion with God, walking and talking with Him like close friends, but sin ruined that for Adam and all his descendants. This face-to-face communion will never be restored this side of heaven.

Sin also separated mankind from the rest of creation. Adam's sin brought suffering and death to everything, and everything began to rebel against man's headship, just as man had rebelled against the headship of God. Because of Adam's sin, all of life now fights against us.

REFLECTING ON THE TEXT

5) How have you witnessed the effects brought about by the separation of sin in your own life? In your marriage? At work? At church?

_____

_____

_____

_____

_____

6) When have you tried to debate with someone who doubted the Word of God? What was the result of the debate?

_____

_____

_____

_____

_____

7) When have you deliberately chosen to sin, even though you knew that it was wrong? If you could do it again today, what would you do differently?

_____

_____

_____

_____

_____

8) When have you tried to "cover up" your sinful behavior? What motivated you to do so? How well did it work?

_____

_____

_____

_____

_____

PERSONAL RESPONSE

9) In what ways have you seen the grace of God in your own life? Give specific examples.

_____

_____

_____

_____

10) What area of temptation might the Lord be asking you to address? What deliberate action of obedience might He be calling you to make?

_____

_____

_____

_____

4

CAIN AND ABEL
Genesis 4:1–8

DRAWING NEAR

Cain and Abel were brothers, but a problem arose in their relationship when God only accepted Abel's sacrifice. How does jealousy play a role in family dynamics? What is typically the end result?

_____

_____

_____

_____

THE CONTEXT

Adam and Eve have left the garden of Eden to begin a new and very different life in a fallen world. Everything has changed: animals have become hostile to them and to one another; thorns and thistles have sprung up where once only edible plants had grown. Worst of all, there is something completely new: suffering and death.

We do not know how much time passed between Adam and Eve's expulsion from the garden and the birth of their first son, Cain, but it probably was not more than a few short years. Some people have suggested that Cain and Abel were twins, though the text does not specifically say so. It is likely, either way, that the two brothers were fairly close in age. It is also probable that Adam and Eve had other children besides Cain and Abel during this time, though they are not specifically mentioned in Genesis. Genesis 4 is not concerned with any other siblings, because the story of Cain and Abel is the central focus.

The context of this chapter suggests that God had explained to Adam and his family how to enter His presence with proper sacrifices. The law of Moses had not yet been given, so the full array of sacrifices and offerings was not yet in practice. However, as we saw in the previous study, God Himself made the first animal sacrifice in the garden of Eden, setting the example for Adam's family of what was required: the life of an innocent animal. Fruits and vegetables just wouldn't suffice.

KEYS TO THE TEXT

Read Genesis 4:1–8, noting the key words and phrases indicated below.

> TWO BROTHERS: *Cain and Abel arrive on the scene. One becomes a farmer, the other a shepherd.*

4:1. ADAM KNEW EVE: This Hebrew word is used in many ways, but most frequently it denotes a deeply intimate knowledge. In this case, it is used to describe the sexual intimacy between man and wife. In the previous chapter of Genesis, it was used in reference to mankind's newfound intimacy with evil. Both of these intimacies bear fruit in this chapter.

CAIN: The name Cain means "to possess." Eve made a pun on the name when she said that she had "acquired a man from the Lord."

ACQUIRED A MAN: Some have suggested this is a reference to the promised Redeemer of mankind—that Eve anticipated Cain would fulfill the promise of God concerning "the seed of the woman" (see Genesis 3:15). If that was the case, she was going to be doubly disappointed.

2. THEN SHE BORE AGAIN: We do not know what other children were given to Adam and Eve during this time, but the text seems to suggest that Cain

and Abel were the first and second born, respectively. We can safely surmise that Adam and Eve had daughters soon after, since both sons were married as adults.

ABEL WAS A KEEPER OF SHEEP: The two oldest professions are farming, which Cain took up, and shepherding, which was Abel's profession. These are the two facets of Adam's original calling prior to the Fall, as he was created to have headship over all creation—caring for the animals and tending the garden of Eden.

> TWO OFFERINGS: *Evidently, Adam and his family understood that God wanted them to bring offerings to Him with some regularity, and what sort of offerings He desired.*

3. IN THE PROCESS OF TIME: This phrase indicates that years had passed—Cain is now a married adult (see verse 17).

CAIN BROUGHT AN OFFERING OF THE FRUIT OF THE GROUND: At first glance, this seems like a legitimate act of worship on Cain's part. After all, he was a farmer, so it would be natural for him to give a tithe of his produce to the Lord as an indication of love and worship. The problem was that Cain did not get to make the rules about what offerings were acceptable before God. Cain knew what God wanted, but he ignored God's command and brought what *he* wanted instead.

4. ABEL ALSO BROUGHT OF THE FIRSTBORN OF HIS FLOCK AND OF THEIR FAT: This also seems natural, since Abel was a shepherd. A closer look, however, reveals a distinction in the wording: Cain brought "an offering of the fruit of the ground," while Abel brought "the firstborn" of his sheep and included "their fat." This suggests a generous gift in that Abel set apart God's portion before selecting his own portion. He chose the very first fruit for God, and he did not stint in his generosity. The fat of the lamb makes it clear that the sheep were sacrificed—they shed their blood and died. This is at the heart of God's chosen offering, as He demonstrated in the garden of Eden. "Without shedding of blood, there is no remission" of sins (Hebrews 9:22).

THE LORD RESPECTED ABEL AND HIS OFFERING: Notice the wording here: God *respected* Abel and his offering. Many theologians today claim that God was not happy with Cain's "heart attitude" when he brought his offering, but this is not supported in the text. It is the offering itself, not the attitude

41

of the one bringing it, that concerns God. The Lord's acceptance of Abel was based on his offering, not on anything that he had said or done.

> TWO RESPONSES FROM GOD: *God accepts Abel's offering, and therefore Abel himself, but He rejects Cain's offering. Cain is in grave danger.*

5. HE DID NOT RESPECT CAIN AND HIS OFFERING: Here again it is the offering that is underscored, not Cain's attitude in bringing it. God's rejection of Cain was based on his offering, not on some preference for one brother over the other. God is no respecter of persons; He demands the correct sacrifice from every human being, regardless of race or background or financial status or upbringing or any other factor. The sacrifice is what opens the way into God's presence, not the person bringing it. There was unquestionably a problem with Cain's attitude, but that attitude *led to* the sin—it was not the primary offense itself.

CAIN WAS VERY ANGRY: This is our first clue to the problem that underlies Cain's sin: he wanted to have his own way. If he had merely been ignorant of God's commands concerning animal sacrifices, he might have been embarrassed, but he would not have grown angry.

HIS COUNTENANCE FELL: Cain pouted. This underscores the fact that he was determined to have his own way. He evidently knew that God wanted a sacrifice of shed blood, but that may have been inconvenient for him; perhaps he only raised crops and did not own any livestock. Yet if he had been sincere in his desire to please God, he would have even then rushed out and secured an animal sacrifice—perhaps trading with his brother in exchange for some of his crops. A person who sincerely desires to please someone else does not become angry and petulant when he discovers what is pleasing to the other person; rather, he goes out of his way to do what is pleasing, even if his first attempt failed.

6. SO THE LORD SAID TO CAIN: If there was any question about Cain's knowledge of what was pleasing to God, it was removed here. Even if Cain had not known previously what sort of sacrifice God desired, he understood now. Notice that God, once again, went out of His way to be reunited with mankind, even to the point of speaking directly to a man who was in danger of error.

GOD'S GRACE: Both Cain and Abel have equal opportunity to find acceptance before God, as the Lord now explains to Cain.

WHY ARE YOU ANGRY: Rather than being repentant for his sinful disobedience, Cain was hostile toward God, whom he could not kill, and jealous of his brother, whom he could kill (see John 3:12; Jude 11).

7. IF YOU DO WELL, WILL YOU NOT BE ACCEPTED? Just as God demands the correct sacrifice from all men, so He also offers His grace and salvation to all men alike—regardless of heritage or social class or any other factor. In Cain's case, "doing well" meant bringing the correct sacrifice before God: a sheep whose blood has been shed. God was calling Cain's attention to the underlying problem in his attitude—stubbornness. God was warning Cain that mankind does not have the right to enter His presence on his own terms—we must accept God's terms or be denied access. Without a suitable offering, Cain faced God's rejection.

SIN LIES AT THE DOOR: Cain's insistence on having his own way led him into stubbornness, and his stubbornness led him into anger. If he continued on this path, he would go through the door of anger into murder. The wild beast of sin lurked just beyond that door, waiting to tear him limb from limb. God urged Cain to turn back from this self-destructive path while he still could.

ITS DESIRE IS FOR YOU, BUT YOU SHOULD RULE OVER IT: This is the same phrase that the Lord used when He explained the curse to Eve (see Genesis 3:16). God was warning Cain that he was in danger of turning the created order upside down—the very sin that Adam committed in Genesis 3. God called on Cain to have lordship over his own emotions and decisions, just as He had called Adam, but Cain's desires were trying to gain mastery over him. The New Testament pictures Satan as a ravenous beast who lurks in dark corners, waiting to pounce on the unwary and rend them limb from limb. "Be sober, be vigilant; because your adversary the devil walks about like a roaring lion, seeking whom he may devour. Resist him, steadfast in the faith, knowing that the same sufferings are experienced by your brotherhood in the world" (1 Peter 5:8–9). God warned Cain of this danger but also exhorted him to vanquish that foe—which Peter addressed when he encouraged us to resist the devil, standing "steadfast in the faith."

GOING DEEPER

Read Hebrews 11:4 and 1 John 3:4–12, noting the key words and phrases indicated below.

> *ABEL STILL SPEAKS: The writer of Hebrews points to Abel as an example of faith—an example that we are called to imitate.*

HEBREWS 11:4. BY FAITH: This is the core of both Cain and Abel's sacrifices: the question of faith. Both men had been told what God demanded for a sacrifice, but only Abel accepted that on faith. Abel had faith that God would keep His word if he obeyed with the correct sacrifice. Cain, however, chose to place his faith in his own efforts and schemes.

A MORE EXCELLENT SACRIFICE: As we've already stated, the difference between Cain and Abel was not in their personalities or talents but in the sacrifice which each brought. God demanded a sacrifice of shed blood—the blood of an innocent lamb. By his faith-filled obedience, Abel became an example for us today. We must be like him, acting in faith that God's final sacrifice shall indeed save us from our sins.

> *CHILDREN OF GOD OR THE DEVIL: John tells us that a Christian's life will be characterized by righteousness and love for others. Those who live like Cain are children of the devil.*

1 JOHN 3:6. DOES NOT SIN: That is, "keep on sinning." The Christian's life is characterized by an ongoing struggle *against* sin, not a compliance *with* sin. This obviously does not mean that Christians never sin; it means that Christians never give up the battle against sin.

WHOEVER SINS HAS NEITHER SEEN HIM NOR KNOWN HIM: Again, that is, "whoever continues to sin," making sin a habit or lifestyle. The person who makes sin his master has not submitted to the lordship of Jesus Christ.

8. OF THE DEVIL: John contrasts the children of God with the children of Satan in terms of their actions. While those who are truly born again reflect the habit of righteousness, Satan's children practice sin.

10. THE CHILDREN OF GOD AND THE CHILDREN OF THE DEVIL: These two types are found in Abel and Cain, respectively. The second half of this verse typifies Cain: he did not practice righteousness, nor did he love his brother.

UNLEASHING THE TEXT

1) Whom have you known that reminded you of Abel? Of Cain?

_____

_____

_____

_____

2) Why do you think Cain stubbornly rejected God's plan of sacrifices? Why did Abel obey?

_____

_____

_____

_____

3) In your opinion, was God's response to Cain too harsh? Why or why not?

_____

_____

_____

_____

4) What should have been Cain's response?

_____

_____

_____

_____

Exploring the Meaning

God is not a respecter of persons. God does not play favorites. He makes the same demand equally to every human on the planet: the demand for an acceptable sacrifice for sin. That sacrifice is the blood of Jesus Christ—and there are *no* exceptions.

Abel found favor in God's eyes for the simple reason that his sacrifice was acceptable to God. He brought a suitable offering for his sin, and God accepted that offering. The same is true for Christians: we find favor in the eyes of God simply because He has seen the blood of Jesus covering our sins. If we did not have that blood covering our lives, we would not be permitted into His presence.

In today's world, it is important that people understand this basic concept of the gospel. There are not "many paths" to God—there is only one way, and that is through the blood of Christ. There are no exceptions.

God's grace is freely available to all, without restrictions. Just as God is no respecter of persons concerning sin, so also He is no respecter of persons concerning grace. Cain had the opportunity to receive God's grace when he brought the wrong sacrifice—and he rejected that opportunity.

Yet even then God did not completely cut him off. As we will see in the next study, even after Cain murdered his brother, God gave him another opportunity to repent and ask for grace. Even the sin of murder can be forgiven!

The truth is that there is no sin that cannot be covered by the blood of Christ. God is eager to extend His grace—without restrictions.

Those who reject God's grace become children of the devil. These are strong words in the eyes of Christians in the West. They sound so judgmental, so harsh and "noninclusive." However, this is the teaching of the New Testament. Cain deliberately rejected God's plan for sacrifices and eventually followed in the footsteps of the devil: he became a liar and a murderer.

What we need to recognize is that there are only two choices: to serve Jesus Christ or to serve the devil. There is no in-between ground, no "gray area," no other option. Those who persistently resist the grace of God will gradually become more and more like the devil, who is their father. The only hope for redemption from this desperately downward spiral is to be reborn into the family of Christ.

REFLECTING ON THE TEXT

5) Is God unjust when He insists that there is only one way to salvation? Why or why not?

_____

_____

_____

_____

6) What does it mean to be a child of God? A child of the devil? What does each look like in practical terms?

_____

_____

_____

_____

_____

47

7) In what ways does it require faith to be like Abel? Why is salvation in Jesus Christ only possible on the basis of faith (rather than on the basis of our good works)?

_____

_____

_____

_____

8) Why would the Lord go out of His way to tell Cain what was wrong with his sacrifice and warn him about his attitude? What does this teach us about the grace of God?

_____

_____

_____

_____

PERSONAL RESPONSE

9) Are you a child of God or a child of the devil? How do you know?

_____

_____

_____

_____

10) Is your approach to God more like Abel's or Cain's? What about your
    approach to the people around you?

_____

_____

_____

_____

5

THE FIRST MURDER
Genesis 4:8–16

DRAWING NEAR

What do you think causes a person to consider murdering another person? Why is murder prevalent even in families?

_____

_____

_____

_____

THE CONTEXT

In the previous study we examined the sad story of Cain and Abel, in which two brothers brought different offerings before the Lord. God rejected Cain's offering, while He accepted Abel's offering—and this made Cain very angry. The end result, as we will see, was that Cain murdered his brother Abel.

This is an actual historical event, chronicled in Genesis 4, involving real people. But the New Testament also uses Cain and Abel as "types," or pictures that illustrate two very different sorts of people. In this study, we will consider Cain as a picture of those who reject the salvation offered by God through

51

Christ, while Abel represents a picture of those who are redeemed through Christ's blood.

The major theme that we will discover is that God's grave warnings to Cain apply equally to mankind today: turn away from your stubbornness and repent of your anger or sin will destroy you. The second theme that we will discover is that the fate of Abel is comparable to the suffering that God calls His people to endure even today.

Keys to the Text

Read Genesis 4:8–16, noting the key words and phrases indicated below.

> MURDER: *God calls on Cain to have lordship over his emotions and decisions, but he is steadfast in his determination to reject God's plan. He prefers to find his own way to God and allows his desires to rule over him. Sin thus bears its final fruit: murder.*

4:8. CAIN TALKED WITH ABEL HIS BROTHER: The interesting thing is that both brothers—the one who had found peace with God and the one who defied God—lived together on a daily basis. When we accept Christ's salvation and become one of His children, He does not whisk us out of this world. We will continue to rub elbows every day with those who love God, those who hate God, and the countless masses who are somewhere in between. (Of course, there is actually no such thing as "in between.")

CAIN ROSE UP: This is the physical action that Cain's heart has been exercising all along: he elevated himself, raising himself above his brother. He was consumed with self-will, raising his own will above God's. This is the very attitude that led him to bring an unacceptable offering before God, and here it led him to raise himself above his brother in deadly violence.

KILLED HIM: Why did Cain murder Abel? "Because his works were evil and his brother's righteous" (1 John 3:12). "But each one is tempted when he is drawn away by his own desires and enticed. Then, when desire has conceived, it gives birth to sin; and sin, when it is full-grown, brings forth death" (James 1:14–15). Jesus warned us that those who follow Him will be hated and persecuted by the world. "If the world hates you, you know that it hated Me before it hated you. If you were of the world, the world would love its own. Yet because you are not of the world, but I chose you out of the world, therefore the world hates you. Remember the word that I said to you, 'A servant is not greater than his master.' If they persecuted Me, they will persecute you. If they kept My word, they will keep yours also" (John 15:18–20).

> COVER-UP: *God confronts Cain with his crime in an effort to lead him to confession and repentance, but Cain prefers to lie.*

9. WHERE IS ABEL YOUR BROTHER? Throughout Genesis—indeed, throughout the entire Bible—we find God working to bring reconciliation with individual men and women. Had Cain confessed his sin at that moment, he would have been restored to God, even after murdering his own brother.

I DO NOT KNOW: Cain's reply to God reveals, in two ways, whom he served. His first statement was a direct lie—he certainly *did* know where his brother was. This reveals that his master was the devil, the father of lies and "a murderer from the beginning" (John 8:44), and that he had sealed his allegiance to him.

AM I MY BROTHER'S KEEPER? Cain's follow-up question—one of the most notorious questions in human history—reveals that he also served himself. In fact, it was Cain's self-serving nature that led him into this deadly trap in the first place. This is the ultimate end for everyone who rejects God's salvation plan. Jesus would one day answer the question Himself in the parable of the good Samaritan (see Luke 10:25–37), and the answer would be *yes.*

> CONSEQUENCES: *Cain's refusal to repent of his sin brings the justice of God upon him. Yet even in this, God continues to show mercy and grace.*

10. THE VOICE OF YOUR BROTHER'S BLOOD CRIES OUT TO ME FROM THE GROUND: In Genesis 3, we heard the voice of God calling gently to Adam in the garden of Eden. Now we hear the outraged voice of creation as it cries out against the horrible, unnatural act of murder. God permits His people to suffer under the hateful hand of the world, but He is carefully aware of all their suffering (see Revelation 6:9–11).

11. YOU ARE CURSED FROM THE EARTH: All of creation would now rebel against Cain, even as Cain rebelled against his Creator.

12. WHEN YOU TILL THE GROUND, IT SHALL NO LONGER YIELD ITS STRENGTH TO YOU: The curse that Adam faced was that his work would involve great toil as the earth resisted his efforts. This curse seemed to go a step further, implying that Cain would never again gain mastery over the environment, no matter how hard he labored.

A FUGITIVE AND A VAGABOND: Here is another element of the curse on Adam that was stepped up a notch in Cain's case. Adam and Eve were expelled from the garden of Eden, but they presumably found another place to settle. Cain, however, would be forced to wander to and fro for the rest of his life, mimicking his spiritual father, the devil, who wanders "to and fro on the earth" (Job 1:7).

13. MY PUNISHMENT IS GREATER THAN I CAN BEAR: Cain pouted and sulked when he didn't get his way. Then he threw a temper tantrum. Then he took out his frustrated rage on his innocent brother. Now he whined. This is the pattern of behavior in people who think too highly of themselves—people who indulge and pamper themselves. This is a frightening indictment of the modern "self-esteem" fetish.

14. ANYONE WHO FINDS ME WILL KILL ME: This shows that the population of the earth was, by this time, greatly increased. It is interesting that Cain listed the three things that God specified in the curse—and then added one of his own. God did not say that Cain would be hunted down and killed, but he seemed to conclude that this would happen. This is one of the most common results of sin: we become afraid and make decisions that are based on fear. This happened to Adam as well when he became afraid of God—the only One who could solve his self-induced problem. Fear moves us away from God rather than toward Him.

15. THE LORD SET A MARK ON CAIN: Though not described here, this mark involved some sort of identifiable sign that Cain's physical life was under divine protection. At the same time, it was a visible reminder of his lifelong shame and guilt.

16. CAIN WENT OUT FROM THE PRESENCE OF THE LORD: What a tragic statement! There is a conclusiveness that suggests that Cain never again entered the presence of God.

UNLEASHING THE TEXT

1) Why did Cain become so angry when God rejected his sacrifice? How might he have chosen to respond differently?

_____

_____

_____

_____

2) Cain and Abel lived together on a daily basis. What sort of person was Cain? What kind of neighbor would he be?

_____

_____

_____

_____

_____

3) How does Cain's response to God after the murder of Abel indicate whom he served in his heart?

_____

_____

_____

_____

4) How was the curse God gave to Cain similar and different from the curse He gave to Adam and Eve? How did God show grace even after pronouncing the curse?

_____

_____

_____

_____

EXPLORING THE MEANING

There is only one way to enter God's presence. Cain's sin was that he insisted on entering God's presence on his own terms. He evidently knew that God demanded an animal sacrifice, but he still brought an offering of fruits and vegetables. Ironically, the Lord would institute "grain offerings" under the law of Moses many years later, but Cain was not given that option. This early sacrifice was a sin offering, intended to represent God's atonement for the sins of mankind. For that, the shed blood of an innocent lamb was required.

God's response to Cain demonstrates that He was determined to show mankind what it would cost to bring redemption. These sacrifices were pictures of the sacrificial death of Jesus Christ, and nothing but the blood of an unblemished lamb would do.

Cain is the archetype of the world's teaching that there are many ways to God—that there are multiple paths to eternal peace and bliss. There are undoubtedly many paths that lead to Christ, but the path to the Father is _only_ through the shed blood of Jesus. All who insist that they can find their own way to God will suffer the same fate as Cain: they will shut themselves out from the presence of God forever.

We must shut out sin when it crouches at our door. Abel's offering was acceptable not just because it was an animal, nor because it was the best of what he had, nor even because it was the culmination of a zealous heart for God, but because it was in every way obediently given according to what God must have revealed. Cain, disdaining the divine instruction, just brought what he wanted to bring: some of his crop.

Rather than being repentant for his sinful disobedience, Cain was violently hostile toward God, whom he could not kill, and jealous of his brother, whom he could kill. God reminded Cain that if he had obeyed Him and offered the animal sacrifices He required, his sacrifices would have been acceptable. He also told Cain that if he chose not to obey His commands, ever-present sin, crouched and waiting to pounce like a lion, would fulfill its desire to overpower him.

Cain had the opportunity to examine his heart and change his path. However, he rejected the wisdom spoken to him by God Himself, rejected doing good, and refused to repent. Sin thus pounced and turned him into a killer.

We are our brother's keeper. The world tells us that we must learn to love ourselves before we can truly love others. The Bible teaches the opposite. In fact, Cain demonstrated that nobody really needs to learn how to love himself; we're born with that capacity. Cain set his own interests above those of his family and God.

We are called to esteem others as *better* than we are (see Philippians 2:3) and to put their interests ahead of our own. When we reverse this truth, we will quickly become frustrated at not getting our own way. This frustration leads to anger and resentment, and these emotions lead to murder. It may not take the form of physically killing another person, but Jesus Himself said that to hate and resent others is to murder them in our hearts (see Matthew 5:21–26).

God gets to make the rules. God's rejection of Cain may seem harsh to modern sensibilities. We might even be tempted to sympathize with Cain and his anger with God for being "so darn picky" about his offering. After all, isn't it the heart attitude that matters? Cain's heart was in the right place . . . wasn't it?

In fact, it wasn't. Cain's attitude was that God should consider Himself blessed for receiving an offering in the first place and not be ungrateful about it. Cain demonstrated the natural thinking of mankind and the world around us: *I get to make the rules for myself, and nobody else is going to dictate how I live.*

This thinking is based on the lie of Satan that we are our own gods. Adam determined that he would make his own decisions in the garden of Eden, even though he knew full well that eating the forbidden fruit would lead to death. It may sound noble to suggest that a person would rather die than live in bondage, but the reality is that mankind can never be truly free unless he is under the headship of his Creator. In fact, man will always be in bondage—either to sin and death or to Christ and eternal life. Paul called himself "a bondservant of Jesus Christ" (Romans 1:1), which reflects the right attitude of God's people.

REFLECTING ON THE TEXT

5) In what ways does the world around us encourage us to commit the sin of Cain—by "doing it our way" and insisting on our own rights?

_____

_____

_____

_____

6) When have you seen this trait in someone else? When have you discovered it in yourself?

_____

_____

_____

_____

_____

7) Do you believe that you must learn to love yourself before you can love others? Before you can love God? How does that thinking compare with what you read in Genesis 4:8–16?

_____

_____

_____

_____

8) What does the world say about how a person gets to heaven? What does it say about the character of God?

_____

_____

_____

_____

PERSONAL RESPONSE

9) Have you submitted to God's way of salvation? If not, what is preventing you from submitting to His will right now?

_____

_____

_____

10) Do you give regularly and generously to God's work? How well are you doing at giving God your very best? Your firstfruits?

_____

_____

_____

_____

6

NOAH AND THE ARK

Genesis 6:5–22

DRAWING NEAR

Noah was a man who stood out in his generation. Who are some people today whom you feel stand out because of their beliefs or character? How do they stand out?

_____

_____

_____

_____

THE CONTEXT

Time has passed yet again, and we are now roughly 1,500 years after creation. Genesis 5 gives a complete genealogy from Adam to Noah, showing that it was approximately 1,056 years from Adam's creation to Noah's birth, and that Noah was 600 years old when God flooded the entire earth. During that time, mankind did not improve.

In fact, Genesis tells us that "the wickedness of man was great in the earth, and that every intent of the thoughts of his heart was only evil continually" (6:5). The wickedness of mankind had indeed become so great that the Lord "was grieved in His heart" (verse 6). Yet in the midst of this great wickedness, there was one man who "found grace in the eyes of the Lord" (verse 8)—a man named Noah.

God selected Noah to become a second Adam—the father of the human race. This honor set Noah apart from every other human being on earth, which indicates that there was something special about him in God's eyes. In this study, we will look more closely at who Noah was so that we can learn to imitate him—that we, too, might be pleasing to God.

KEYS TO THE TEXT

Read Genesis 6:5–22, noting the key words and phrases indicated below.

A WICKED WORLD: Mankind has so degenerated into the depths of wickedness that God declares He is sorry He made humans.

6:5. EVERY INTENT OF THE THOUGHTS OF HIS HEART WAS ONLY EVIL CONTINUALLY: This is a strong statement concerning the true nature of man's heart. James tells us that man's sinful behavior begins in his thought life (see James 1:14–15). Jeremiah states, "The heart is deceitful above all things, and desperately wicked; who can know it?" (17:9). This is a recurrent teaching of Scripture, and it again defies the world's misguided notion that mankind is inherently good.

6. HE WAS GRIEVED IN HIS HEART: This is actually a moving insight into the character of God—He is capable of feeling sorrow and grief. What moves Him to grief is the sinfulness of His special creature, man, whom He designed and created to hold a special degree of communion with Himself. He is grieved that man now spends his energies and talents devising new ways to defy his Creator.

ONE SET APART: Yet there is one man in that wicked generation whose life is different—one man who finds favor in the eyes of God.

8. BUT NOAH FOUND GRACE IN THE EYES OF THE LORD: The name Noah means "rest." His father prophesied at his birth: "This one will comfort

us concerning our work and the toil of our hands, because of the ground which the Lord has cursed" (Genesis 5:29). In the midst of the world's unprecedented wickedness, Noah stood out as radically different. This forces us to ask *what* was different about him. What was it about Noah that brought him the favor and grace of God?

9. NOAH WAS A JUST MAN: Here is the beginning of our answer. This statement suggests that there was little justice in the society around him—wicked men were being rewarded and innocent men punished, much as it is in the West today. But Noah pursued justice in his dealings with family and neighbors.

PERFECT IN HIS GENERATIONS: That is, Noah was blameless among his contemporaries. The same was said of Daniel, who kept his life so blameless that his enemies could not find any charge to bring against him (see Daniel 6:4).

NOAH WALKED WITH GOD: This is the core reason as to why Noah was able to be just and blameless in the midst of a wicked generation: he walked with God. The Hebrew word translated "walked" is used to mean "come," "go," "walk," or "proceed." Figuratively it means to live or die, or the manner of one's life. In other words, Noah's entire life was characterized by the presence of God. Noah made all his decisions, conducted all his affairs, and acted out his everyday life with the conscious attitude that he was in the presence of God.

SALVATION: God had determined to get rid of the corruption on earth by sending a great flood. However, He promised to keep Noah and His family safe in the ark.

13. I WILL DESTROY THEM WITH THE EARTH: "Destroy" did not mean annihilation but rather referred to the Flood judgment, both of the earth and its inhabitants.

14. MAKE YOURSELF AN ARK: While the ark was not designed for beauty or speed, these dimensions provided extraordinary stability in the tumultuous floodwaters. The ark had three stories, each fifteen feet high, and each deck was equipped with various rooms (literally "nests").

PITCH: Pitch was a resin substance used to seal the seams and cracks in the wood.

16. WINDOW: The "window" may have actually been a low wall around the flat roof to catch water for all on the ark.

18. BUT I WILL ESTABLISH MY COVENANT WITH YOU: Unlike the rest of the created order that God was about to destroy, Noah and his family would not only to be preserved but would also enjoy the provision and protection of a covenant relationship with God. This is the first mention of covenant in Scripture.

UNLEASHING THE TEXT

1) What does it mean to be *just*? How can a normal person show justice in everyday situations? Give some examples.

_____

_____

_____

_____

2) What does it mean to be *blameless* in your generation? List some people you know who would fit that description.

_____

_____

_____

_____

3) Noah's name meant "rest." How did he live up to that name? In what ways did others find rest through him? How did even God find rest through him?

_____

_____

_____

_____

4) Why did Noah find grace in God's eyes? How was he different from the
   world around him?

_____

_____

_____

_____

EXPLORING THE MEANING

God is both merciful and just. Christians sometimes tend to focus on the mercy
and grace of God at the expense of His justice. There is no question that God's
mercy is "new every morning" (Lamentations 3:23) and that His grace extends
to all people, yet we must not miss the fact that He is also perfectly just. It is easy
for mankind to forget this fact, because God is so patient and quick to forgive.

The justice of God will one day fall in full measure on mankind's sin and
wickedness. The people of Noah's day had never witnessed God's justice and
wrath and therefore had deluded themselves into thinking that they never
would. This is a deadly misconception, for God's wrath is only "waiting," hold-
ing itself in check to afford mankind the full amount of time for repentance
and salvation.

The New Testament warns us that the end times will come when life on
earth is "as the days of Noah were" (Matthew 24:37). God ultimately promised
Noah that He would never again destroy the earth by a flood (see Genesis 9:11),
but He has also promised that the day is coming when He will destroy the earth
by fire (see 2 Peter 3:10–11; Revelation 20:9).

God is faithful to those who walk with Him. The world had grown so wicked
and corrupt in Noah's time that God could no longer endure mankind's presence. He determined to destroy *all* living creatures—not just man alone. Yet in
the midst of this, He found one man who was walking faithfully with Him, and
He preserved both him and his family. They never even got wet.

This suggests that God is always searching diligently—not to find sinners for punishment, but to find righteous men and women for reward. Even if there are only two or three righteous, He will always be faithful to protect and preserve them from His wrath. The same was true for Lot and his family, who were rescued out of Sodom prior to its destruction (see Genesis 19:1–17).

We are called to walk with God. Genesis emphasizes repeatedly that Noah obeyed God in all things. He was still a sinner, which becomes evident in a later chapter, yet his life was characterized by a steadfast determination to obey God. Noah also demonstrated what God desires in His people: a heart that is steadfast in obedience. Noah did not question God or argue against His plan; he just did what God told him to do. He had never seen a rainstorm or a flood any more than the other people in his world, yet he chose to be different and obey in faith.

Noah is only one of many in Scripture who "walked with God" (Genesis 6:9). These were men and women whose lives were characterized by a consciousness of God's presence at all times. Everywhere they went, they walked as though God were beside them. Every word they spoke and every action of their lives was marked with the recognition that God was watching and listening.

This lifestyle is attainable by all who have accepted Jesus as Savior, because we have the Holy Spirit dwelling within us—and He desires this lifestyle for us even more than we do ourselves! Noah demonstrated the key to this: trust and obey. He was quick to worship God, quick to believe His word, and quick to obey. This is still the way to walk with God, even in the twenty-first century.

REFLECTING ON THE TEXT

5) In what ways is the world around you today similar to the world of Noah's day? In what ways might it be different?

_____

_____

_____

_____

6) What disciplines do you have in your life that help you walk with God? What stumbling blocks do you have that interfere?

_____

_____

_____

_____

_____

7) Which is easier for you: trusting or obeying? Why? How can Noah's example help you to do both?

_____

_____

_____

_____

_____

8) When have you been deeply saddened or grieved by the actions of a loved one? How might this give you insight into God's response to your sin?

_____

_____

_____

_____

_____

PERSONAL RESPONSE

9) How frequently do you spend time alone worshiping God? How frequently do you spend time worshiping God with others?

_____

_____

_____

_____

10) Are you, like Noah, always quick to worship God, believe His word, and obey? Why or why not? What changes do you need to make to do this better?

_____

_____

_____

_____

7

THE GREAT FLOOD
Genesis 7:1–8:22

DRAWING NEAR

Natural disasters happen in our world on a regular basis. How do you think most people react when they experience these "acts of God"?

_____

_____

_____

_____

THE CONTEXT

Modern science tells us that mankind is getting better and smarter and wiser all the time. However, as we saw in the last study, the 1,500 years from the time of creation to the time of Noah reveals that this is not true. The human race had become so depraved that God regretted creating it. He actually determined in His heart to destroy it.

If that were the end of the story, you would not be reading this book at present, because you would not exist. Fortunately for all of us, God found one righteous man in the midst of this wicked generation named Noah—a man who feared Him and did all that He commanded. He selected Noah to build an ark to save him and his family, and in this way he became a second father to the human race.

It took Noah approximately one hundred years to build the ark. During this time, he was also busy warning the people around him that God was about to send a worldwide judgment on the earth. The ark had room to accommodate all who wanted to escape that judgment—but nobody listened.

Keys to the Text

Read Genesis 7:1–8:22, noting the key words and phrases indicated below.

Building a Boat: In Genesis 6, God commands Noah to build an ark. It takes Noah a century to build it, during which time he preaches about God's coming judgment.

7:2. Seven each of every clean animal: We traditionally picture Noah collecting two of every living animal on earth—a male and a female—but this is not accurate. God commanded him to collect seven (or, more likely, seven pairs) of every clean animal, and two (a pair) of every unclean animal. (See Leviticus 11 and Deuteronomy 14 for further information concerning clean and unclean animals.)

4. Seven more days: God had already allowed 100 years for the people to repent. Noah was "a preacher of righteousness" (2 Peter 2:5) to the world around him, while "the Divine longsuffering waited" (1 Peter 3:20) as he built the ark. Now God would allow one more week of opportunity for others to repent and find salvation on the ark. Nobody responded.

I will cause it to rain on the earth forty days and forty nights: Prior to this time, it had never rained on earth—at least not in any large quantity. This is probably part of the reason why people mocked Noah as he built the ark, saying, "Such a thing has never happened before—therefore we are confident that it never will." This foolish thinking is still prevalent in the world today.

I will destroy from the face of the earth all living things that I have made: Some people surmise that the earth was originally surrounded by a canopy of water vapor. This canopy would have shielded the earth from the sun's destructive rays and contributed to the great life spans recorded in Genesis. If such a canopy did exist, it certainly contained enough water to flood the earth. Added to this was a great quantity of subterranean waters that belched forth from below the earth's surface. Every living creature died, with the exception of fish ("all that was on the dry land," Genesis 7:22).

5. NOAH DID ACCORDING TO ALL THAT THE LORD COMMANDED HIM: This is the practical element involved in "walking with God." Certainly a man who walks with God will spend time reading His Word, communing in prayer, meeting with others who are like-minded, and so forth. But at the core of this is one word: *obedience*. Noah's life was characterized by obedience to God. Whatever God told him to do, he did it—exactly as God described. In this, Noah is a type of Christ as well as a second Adam: a man whose life was characterized by complete obedience to the Father.

ALL ABOARD: Noah and his family get inside the ark, and God closes the door. Soon there will be no safe place on earth, except inside the ark.

6. NOAH WAS 600 YEARS OLD: The genealogies of those who lived prior to the Flood record incredibly long lives—Methuselah, the oldest man in the Bible, lived to be 969 (see Genesis 5:27). The life spans of those born after the Flood, however, are dramatically shorter, which lends some credence to the concept that the earth had been surrounded by a water-vapor canopy.

11. IN THE SECOND MONTH: The dates and timing of the Flood are meticulous and specific, which indicates that Moses accepted it as an actual, historical event. This is not a myth or a fable; it is literal history. The entire flood lasted one year and ten days from beginning to end (see Genesis 7:11–8:14).

THE FOUNTAINS OF THE GREAT DEEP: Waters surged up from underground and poured violently down from the heavens. This was undoubtedly accompanied by earthquakes, as the subterranean waters broke through the surface of the earth. This is a picture of a worldwide catastrophe, not an event restricted to one geographical area.

13. ON THE VERY SAME DAY NOAH ... ENTERED THE ARK: As we have seen, God gave mankind every possible opportunity to repent, up to the very

last minute. God reaches out in grace and mercy to mankind constantly—but the time does come when His judgment falls. He is both merciful *and* just.

15. THEY WENT INTO THE ARK TO NOAH: This suggests that God brought the animals to Noah; he did not have to go around the earth collecting two of every species.

16. AND THE LORD SHUT HIM IN: God Himself shut the door of the ark, and only He could open it again. This suggests that the door had been standing open all this time—a literal open door to any who would go in to salvation. However, when the time was completely fulfilled, God at last shut that door— and it would never again open to those on the outside." Now is the day of salvation" (2 Corinthians 6:2), but this day will not last forever.

THE WATERS RISE: The entire planet is covered with water so deep that it covers the mountain tops.

18. THE ARK MOVED ABOUT ON THE SURFACE OF THE WATERS: The New Testament uses the ark as a picture of God's plan of salvation and the church. Here we see the horrible judgment of God's wrath being poured forth on the entire globe, destroying all life on the planet, while God's people remain safely apart from that destruction. Not one bit of God's judgment fell on Noah's family. So it will be for God's church when His final judgment is poured forth on the earth.

20. THE MOUNTAINS WERE COVERED: Fifteen cubits would be more than 22 feet deep, meaning that the highest mountain was submerged under at least 22 feet of water. The ark eventually landed on Mount Ararat, which is 17,000 feet high. Again, these simple statistics prove beyond any doubt that this water covered the entire planet—not just a small geographical region as some have claimed.

GOD'S WRATH ABATES: God's nature demands both mercy and judgment. However, now that His judgment has been appeased, His mercy comes to the forefront.

8:1. GOD REMEMBERED NOAH: This does not mean that God had forgotten Noah, but that His wrath against the wickedness of mankind was now appeased. He "remembered" His divine mercy toward mankind, as His divine judgment had now been fulfilled, and turned His attention to getting Noah situated in the post-Flood earth.

GOD MADE A WIND TO PASS OVER THE EARTH: Here we see some repetitions of God's original creation of earth. His Spirit hovered over the waters during creation, and now He sends "a wind" to pass over the waters. The word for "wind" is the same as for "spirit."

4. THE MOUNTAINS OF ARARAT: These are in the region of the Caucasus, the tallest peaks in modern-day Turkey.

7. RAVEN: The raven is a carrion eater, a bird of death. It undoubtedly found much rancid flesh to feed on, but there was no dry ground suitable for it to roost. It kept going "to and fro," that is, out of the ark window and back again.

8. HE ALSO SENT OUT FROM HIMSELF A DOVE: A dove is much more selective in its food choices than a raven. The dove's choice of food would indicate that new life had begun to grow and that Noah and his family could also survive outside the ark.

11. FRESHLY PLUCKED OLIVE LEAF: This indicates that the waters had subsided to the point that trees were dry and putting forth fresh leaves. Appropriately, the dove and the olive branch have endured throughout history as symbols of peace.

13. NOAH REMOVED THE COVERING OF THE ARK: This was probably a window or hatch of some sort. Noah did not leave the ark until God commanded him to do so (see Genesis 8:16).

NOAH WORSHIPED: Noah not only obeys God but also worships Him. These characteristics set him apart from his generation and reveal the secret to his strong relationship with God.

20. NOAH BUILT AN ALTAR TO THE LORD: Noah and his family had been cooped up inside the ark for 378 days. They had not felt sunshine, touched dry land, or lived any kind of normal existence during that time, but the first thing Noah did after leaving the ark was build an altar to worship God. Most people would rush about building shelter for themselves, gathering food and so forth, and perhaps even plan a party. But Noah was a man who walked with God, and his first thought was to worship.

21. THE LORD SMELLED A SOOTHING AROMA: God's justice had been satisfied and His anger was abated. Once again, Noah gives us a picture of Christ, whose perfect sacrifice for sin would later be the final offering—the sacrifice that made complete atonement for the sins of man and opened the way to removing the curse.

UNLEASHING THE TEXT

1) What brought God's wrath on the earth?

_____

_____

_____

_____

2) Why did God destroy all living things rather than just mankind?

_____

_____

_____

_____

3) What does this event teach you about God's character? About man's character?

_____

_____

_____

_____

_____

4) Why did God select Noah? What two characteristics did he possess that made him different from the people around him?

_____

_____

_____

_____

_____

EXPLORING THE MEANING

God always rescues His people from His wrath. When the day of God's wrath in the future comes on the earth, He will first remove His people. His involvement with Noah millennia ago serves as a vivid illustration of His future involvement with the church. Just as He kept Noah and his family safe above the floodwaters, so He will keep His church safe from the fullness of His wrath.

God is completely faithful to His people and His promises, and He will always preserve His church. This certainly does not mean that God's people will not suffer, but that suffering will be only a temporary state, whereas God's wrath brings eternal damnation and separation from His presence. Noah and his family suffered some deprivation and discomfort inside the ark, but God kept them alive and safe during the terrible outpouring of His wrath on the earth.

The ark is a picture of Christ and His church. Peter used the ark as an illustration of the salvation that is found in Jesus Christ (see 1 Peter 3). It took time for the ark to be brought to completion, and during that time God had His prophet speaking boldly to the people of earth, warning them of the coming destruction. The same is true of Christ's church, though the time of judgment has not yet arrived. There is still time today for the lost to find salvation.

Note that Noah and his family were kept safe only by entering the body of the ark. There was no other way to survive the Flood. In the same way, mankind can only find refuge from God's coming wrath inside the body of Christ. There is no other way of salvation available to mankind.

The body of the ark bore the wrath that God rained down on creation, but those inside it remained completely dry. The full wrath of God against sin and death ultimately poured down on Christ as He hung upon the cross, but those who have been redeemed by Christ will never feel one drop of the Father's just wrath.

Noah, the ark, and the Flood are literal, historical facts. This Flood did occur, just as described in Genesis. Noah was a real man who literally built a real ark, and all people on earth today are descended from him.

There are many today, even within the body of Christ, who try to claim that this passage is merely a myth or fable. They state that the Flood narrative is an allegorical story that is intended to be read metaphorically for some "deeper truths," not a historical account of actual events. But the Bible as a whole does not treat it that way. Jesus Himself spoke of the Flood as an actual event and of Noah as a real person.

There are certainly symbols in this passage that help us better understand the character of God and the work of Christ, but we must not lose sight of the fact that these people and events were real. If modern science claims that they never happened, we must choose to place our faith in God's Word—not in the teachings of men.

God loves our worship. The Bible frequently refers to our prayers as a "sweet aroma" to God. Just as men love the smell of their favorite treats being baked by their loving wives, and women love the aroma of a bouquet of flowers brought home by loving husbands, so God loves the sweet fragrance of praise and worship given freely by the people He has redeemed at great cost.

Noah set the example for us. Remember that the *first* thing that he did when he stepped off the ark—even after a year of harrowing ordeal—was to build an altar and worship God. This should always be the first response of God's people, whether we are coming out of a time of suffering, receiving a great blessing, or merely going about our humdrum daily lives.

Worship was central in Noah's life, and it should be the same with God's people today.

REFLECTING ON THE TEXT

5) How have you witnessed the mercy of God in your own life? How have you seen—or not seen—the justice of God?

_____

_____

_____

_____

_____

6) How does the fact that God is both merciful and just move you to a deeper worship of Him?

_____

_____

_____

_____

7) If you had been on board the ark, how would you have felt about the friends and family that you knew were outside drowning? How is your urgency to share the gospel impacted by God's coming judgment?

_____

_____

_____

_____

8) When have you seen God protecting you or your loved ones? What part did you play in that protection? What part was beyond your control?

_____

_____

_____

_____

_____

PERSONAL RESPONSE

9) In what ways has God called you to believe His word on faith, despite the beliefs of the world around you?

_____

_____

_____

_____

10) What things in your life might be a "sweet aroma" to God? What might be a nasty stench? What do you need to do for your life to smell better?

_____

_____

_____

_____

8

THE FIRST COVENANT
Genesis 9:1–17

DRAWING NEAR

A "covenant" is a commitment or agreement between two parties. What kinds of covenants do we enter in today? How are those similar or dissimilar to God's covenants or promises to His people?

_____

_____

_____

_____

THE CONTEXT

Throughout Genesis, God made numerous covenants with men. Some of these covenants were *conditional*, in the sense that God's people had something to do if the contract was to remain binding. Other covenants were *unconditional*, in that God would keep His end of the bargain regardless of what His people did. But all of the covenants had this in common: they revealed some aspect of God's nature, and they displayed the hopeless situation that mankind was in.

We saw this utter hopelessness in God's first "covenant" with mankind in Genesis 3:16–19, which was not so much a covenant as a curse. There was absolutely nothing that Adam and Eve could do to reverse the curse, which reveals mankind's hopeless state. Yet right from the beginning, God promised a Deliverer who would come through "the seed of the woman" to redeem mankind. This revealed, also from the beginning, the nature of God's loving and gracious plan for man's redemption.

In this study, we will look at the covenant that God later made with Noah after the Flood. In so doing, we will discover some important aspects of mankind's sin nature and be encouraged by glimpses of God's perfect nature.

KEYS TO THE TEXT

Read Genesis 9:1–17, noting the key words and phrases indicated below.

AFTER THE FLOOD: The floodwaters have receded, and God has set Noah and his family safely on dry ground. Now God pronounces a blessing on Noah.

9:1. BLESSED NOAH ... BE FRUITFUL AND MULTIPLY, AND FILL THE EARTH: God blessed Noah and recommissioned him to fill the earth, just as previously He had instructed Adam and Eve to fill the earth (see Genesis 1:28).

2. THE FEAR OF YOU: Man's relationship to the animals appears to have changed, in that man is free to eat animals for sustenance.

4. BUT YOU SHALL NOT EAT FLESH WITH ITS LIFE: Raw blood was not to be consumed as food, for it symbolically represented life. To shed blood symbolically represented death. The blood of animals, representing their life, was not to be eaten. It was, in fact, that blood which God designed to be a covering for sin (see Leviticus 17:11).

5. FROM THE HAND OF EVERY BEAST ... HAND OF MAN: God invoked capital punishment on every animal or man who took human life unlawfully.

6. FOR IN THE IMAGE OF GOD: The reason man could kill animals, but neither animals nor man could kill man, was because man alone was created in God's image.

THE COVENANT: After blessing Noah, God now voluntarily commits Himself to an eternal covenant with mankind and the whole earth.

9. I ESTABLISH MY COVENANT WITH YOU: This is the first covenant between God and mankind and is known as the Noahic covenant (see also Genesis 6:18). It was an unconditional covenant, established by God at His own initiative. He was basing it solely on His own nature; man's actions had no part in it.

10. WITH EVERY LIVING CREATURE: God's loving concern extends to all of creation, even though mankind is special in His eyes.

11. NEVER AGAIN SHALL THERE BE A FLOOD: God promised that there would never again be a flood that covers the entire planet. Prophets of future catastrophe, such as global warming, often claim that there may be a major flood (because of melting ice caps and other factors) if mankind doesn't do something quickly, but God has promised otherwise. It is important to note, however, that the Lord did *not* promise that the earth would exist forever.

12. THE SIGN OF THE COVENANT: The rainbow is the perpetual, symbolic reminder of this covenant promise, just as circumcision of all males would be for the Abrahamic covenant (see Genesis 17:10–11).

PERPETUAL GENERATIONS: This covenant between God and man shall last forever—even longer than the earth itself will last.

14. WHEN I BRING A CLOUD OVER THE EARTH: This essentially would mean at every moment of every day, since there is never a time when clouds are not moving across some portion of the planet's face. God was saying that He would never forget, not even for a moment, the covenant that He had made.

15. I WILL REMEMBER: This is not simple recognition, but God's commitment to keep the promise.

16. THE EVERLASTING COVENANT: God's covenant with Noah was the first of five divinely originated covenants in Scripture that are explicitly described as "everlasting." The term "everlasting" can mean either to the end of time, and/or through eternity future. It never looks back to eternity past. Of the six explicitly mentioned covenants of this kind in Scripture, only the Mosaic or old covenant was nullified.

UNLEASHING THE TEXT

1) What does this passage in Genesis 9:1–17 demonstrate about God's intentions for mankind?

_____

_____

_____

_____

_____

2) What does this passage demonstrate about God's character?

_____

_____

_____

_____

_____

3) Why might God have chosen the rainbow as the symbol of His covenant? Why not sunshine or rain clouds?

_____

_____

_____

_____

4) Why did God choose to make an unconditional covenant with Noah? What is implicit in His promise toward the earth? What is not?

_____

_____

_____

_____

EXPLORING THE MEANING

Every human who has ever lived was born a sinner. God cannot tolerate any sin—no matter how small or insignificant. Consider the sin of Adam: all he did was eat a piece of fruit! Yet this act of deliberate rebellion was so monumental, so heinous and horrible, that God cursed His creation and cast mankind from His presence.

No person who has ever lived, apart from Jesus Christ, has been free of sin. Every descendant of Adam has been a sinner from birth. There are no exceptions to this rule. (This, incidentally, is the reason why Jesus had to be born of a virgin, for no human being could have been His father—only God can bring forth a sinless human being.) When Adam sinned, there was no hope of any human being ever entering the presence of God again. Yet God found a way!

God always makes the overture of grace. God hates sin—but He loves to save sinners. He demonstrated this love after Adam had disobeyed Him by deliberately coming into the presence of sinners in the garden of Eden. Consider what a role reversal this was. God had paraded the animals before Adam, because Adam was their caretaker; yet now God Himself, the Creator and Sustainer of the universe, was humbling Himself by presenting Himself before a sinful man!

Likewise, we observe in the story of Noah and the Flood that even though God had decided to wipe out the wickedness on the earth, He made provision to save those who repented of their sins. As we have seen, God waited

83

approximately 100 years from the time Noah started building the ark to the time the first rains fell. The people could have listened to Noah and been saved from the devastation to come, but no one accepted God's free gift of mercy.

God will make His mercy available as long as the earth endures. This principle is double-edged. On one side, God has sworn by Himself that He will not destroy His creation by a flood. He is withholding His hand of judgment from the earth, making His grace and mercy freely available to any person who will confess his sin and sincerely believe in the Lord Jesus Christ.

On the other side, God's judgment *shall* come. God has promised that one day He *will* destroy this world. God's grace and mercy are freely available to all people, yet sinners can continually reject that grace. Those who die without repenting from their sin and turning to God shall find that they have no further hope of grace or salvation.

It is for this reason that Paul warned us, "Behold, now is the accepted time; behold, now is the day of salvation" (2 Corinthians 6:2).

REFLECTING ON THE TEXT

5) After the Flood, God told Noah that the fear of humans would be on every animal on the earth. How was this different from the situation in the garden of Eden?

_____

_____

_____

_____

_____

_____

6) What requirements did God establish with Noah related to eating the flesh of animals? Why did He impose these restrictions?

_____

_____

_____

_____

_____

7) How does God's covenant with Noah apply to the world today? What implications does it have concerning our environment (see Genesis 8:21–22)?

_____

_____

_____

_____

8) What did the Lord do to bring reconciliation with mankind after the Flood? What does this teach about God's desire to be reconciled to all people?

_____

_____

_____

_____

PERSONAL RESPONSE

9) What is your view of sin? Are you as disgusted by it as God is? Why or why not?

_____

_____

_____

_____

10) Are there some areas in your life where you are more tolerant of sin? If so, what can you do to turn those areas over to God?

_____

_____

_____

_____

9

THE SONS OF NOAH
Genesis 9:18–29

DRAWING NEAR

In the story of Noah after the Flood, we read how his youngest son, Ham, mocked his father. In what ways does gossip and shaming others play a major role in our society?

_____

_____

_____

_____

THE CONTEXT

We have been examining Noah in several studies, but we should remember that he was not alone on the ark: he was accompanied by his wife, his three sons, and his sons' wives. (And lots of animals, too, of course.)

In this study, we pick up after the Flood, when Noah and his family are settling themselves into the "new world." They are the only human beings alive on the entire planet, which must have been a major source of stress for them. They had climbed into the ark a year or so earlier, and now all their neighbors, friends, and extended family—whom they had watched gather at the door in mocking laughter—were dead. Any sense of vindication probably evaporated quickly as they realized that there was no one else alive to talk to anywhere on earth.

And, as we will see in this passage, the one piece of baggage that they had not left behind was their sinful nature.

KEYS TO THE TEXT

Read Genesis 9:18–27, noting the key words and phrases indicated below.

> *MY THREE SONS: Noah had three sons named Shem, Ham, and Japheth, who fathered the three major "people groups" found in the world today.*

9:18. SHEM, HAM, AND JAPHETH: Genesis 10:21 in the *New King James Version* tells us Japheth was the oldest, then Shem, then Ham. Other translations reverse the first two—making Shem the firstborn and Japheth the middle son. Regardless, every human alive today is descended from Noah, and these three sons fathered the three major "people groups" in the world.

HAM WAS THE FATHER OF CANAAN: The Canaanites would be one of Israel's greatest enemies in later years. The reason for this comment becomes apparent very soon.

19. FROM THESE THE WHOLE EARTH WAS POPULATED: Modern anthropology has determined that all races on earth are derived from three "people groups." It's always nice when modern science confirms what the Bible says, but we don't need the world's endorsement to believe the Bible. God's Word tells us that all people are descended from the sons of Noah, and we therefore know that it is true.

20. NOAH BEGAN TO BE A FARMER: It's interesting that the two farmers mentioned in Genesis are Cain and Noah. Noah's vineyard is going to get him into trouble, just as Cain's fruit did.

HE PLANTED A VINEYARD: This seems a rather frivolous sort of farming compared to planting more substantial food sources such as vegetables or grain. Of course, we are not told where Noah settled; it is quite possible that the terrain was unsuitable for anything else.

NOAH'S LAPSE: This is the one recorded failure in the life of Noah, a great man who walked with God. Yet even this one sin has dramatic consequences.

21. HE DRANK OF THE WINE AND WAS DRUNK: Noah's lapse from obedience reminds us that even the most faithful men of God are still sinners and that we are never free from the danger of falling into trouble. Sometimes the greatest temptations come after significant victories, as is the case with Noah here.

BECAME UNCOVERED IN HIS TENT: Evidently Noah drank himself into a stupor and fell asleep in his tent. He may have taken off his clothes because of the heat or been involuntarily exposed due to drunkenness.

HAM'S SIN: Noah's youngest son, Ham, is delighted to see his father act "like a normal human being" and gloats at his father's state.

22. HAM, THE FATHER OF CANAAN: Moses repeated this phrase several times, which demonstrates that it was important for his audience to remember that the Canaanites were descended from Ham. Moses was probably writing this book during the forty years of wandering in the desert, so he may have been preparing the people of Israel for the day when they would enter the Promised Land—and be confronted with a host of pagan Canaanites.

SAW THE NAKEDNESS OF HIS FATHER: This passage seems strange to modern Westerners, and some have attempted to read in all sorts of bizarre behavior on the part of Ham. Such readings are unjustified—the text here is quite straightforward: Ham entered his father's tent and stood gazing at his drunken father. Perhaps he stood and mocked. Perhaps he was pleased to see the great man finally commit some act of sin and folly. We don't know because we aren't told, but we do know that Ham failed to do the one thing that he should have done—cover his father and leave.

TOLD HIS TWO BROTHERS OUTSIDE: Ham evidently rushed out of the tent, eager to tell the others what he had seen. The implication seems to be that he was expecting his brothers to come back into the tent with him and join him in mocking their father. Ham's sin was not in *seeing* his father in this shameful state—that part was Noah's fault for becoming drunk. The sin was that Ham did not honor his father by covering him up and keeping silent. Instead, he went out looking for others to join him in his mockery.

HAM'S BROTHERS ARE FAITHFUL: Shem and Japheth, unlike their younger brother, Ham, are honorable and take great pains to cover their father's disgrace.

23. BUT SHEM AND JAPHETH TOOK A GARMENT: Ham's brothers demonstrated the proper response to the situation: they covered their father's shame. Remember that this was God's response to the nakedness and shame of Adam and Eve—He made coverings for them from animal skins (see Genesis 3:21).

WENT BACKWARD: Shem and Japheth demonstrated genuine integrity in this action. It would have been easy for them to excuse a glance at their father's drunken condition, just as it is easy to indulge in some gloating even as we try to help others. However, these two sons took extreme pains to avoid even looking at Noah's disgrace. "He who covers a transgression seeks love, but he who repeats a matter separates friends" (Proverbs 17:9).

COVERED THE NAKEDNESS OF THEIR FATHER: This is the basic principle that this event illustrates: we are called on to assist others in covering their shame. It is easy to gossip about a person who has fallen into sin or hardship, and it can even make us feel better about ourselves. But God wants His people to *cover* each other's shame, not expose it. "Brethren, if a man is overtaken in any trespass, you who are spiritual restore such a one in a spirit of gentleness, considering yourself lest you also be tempted" (Galatians 6:1).

NOAH'S BLESSINGS AND CURSE: Noah pronounces two great blessings and one great curse on his sons. The results of these pronouncements can still be seen today.

24. KNEW WHAT HIS YOUNGER SON HAD DONE TO HIM: We should remember that when a Christian falls into shame and disgrace, that shame

will not last forever—the blood of Christ has already covered the transgression. This should encourage us when we fall into trouble ourselves and serve as a sober reminder when we are tempted to gossip. "And above all things have fervent love for one another, for 'Love will cover a multitude of sins'" (1 Peter 4:8).

25. CURSED BE CANAAN: At first glance, this seems a harsh response to a fairly minor offense. After all, Noah was cursing Ham's descendants, not just Ham himself. However, it underscores the seriousness of Ham's sin and reminds us of the tragic fact that one man's sin will affect others. Remember that Adam's sin was extremely minor by modern standards, yet his curse has carried down to every one of his descendants—that is, every human who has ever lived (with the exception of Christ, who through the Virgin Birth was *not* a son of Adam).

A SERVANT OF SERVANTS: This does not mean that all of Ham's descendants would become slaves (since the curse only refers to the descendants of Canaan). But it does mean that the descendants of Shem—the Israelites—were destined to conquer the Canaanites. This was a needed reminder to the people of Israel as they prepared to enter the Promised Land.

26. BLESSED BE THE LORD, THE GOD OF SHEM: It is interesting that Noah blessed Japheth personally but not Shem—rather, he blessed Shem's God. This is our first clue that Shem's line would be the chosen seed for the Messiah, for it is through Shem's descendants that God would be blessed by showing forth His plan of salvation for all mankind. The people of Israel were chosen not for *their* blessing but for the blessing of God. It was through Israel that God chose to display His character to the world. Similarly, as Christians we are chosen not for our own blessing but for the blessing of God, and we demonstrate to the world around us that the Creator is still working to redeem mankind.

27. MAY GOD ENLARGE JAPHETH: Noah was saying may Japheth's descendants grow to fill and populate the earth. This blessing has come true, as most of the world's people today are descended from Japheth.

MAY HE DWELL IN THE TENTS OF SHEM: Despite the great population of Japheth's descendants, the greatest blessing will still be found in the descendants of Shem. Again, this is undeniably the case, as Jesus Himself came through the line of Shem.

UNLEASHING THE TEXT

1) Imagine what life must have been like for Noah and his family when they first got off the ark. How might you have responded if you had been there?

_____

_____

_____

_____

2) How did Ham respond to his father's indiscretion? How did Shem and Japheth's response differ from Ham's? What was their motivation?

_____

_____

_____

_____

3) How might Ham have responded in a more appropriate manner?

_____

_____

_____

_____

4) Why was it important for the sons to cover their father's shameful condition?

_____

_____

_____

_____

_____

EXPLORING THE MEANING

God's people are called to cover sin, not to gloat or take pleasure in it. The main purpose of this story in Genesis is to introduce the Canaanites as a people who, from the very beginning, were under a divine curse. They were a people marked by sinful corruption, not unlike their forefather Ham in this story, and one day the Israelites would conquer them. Yet there is perhaps an extended principle for Christian living that might be derived from this shocking account, based on the honorable actions of Shem and Japheth.

Ham found his father in a drunken condition and took pleasure in it. He immediately went out and urged his brothers to join him in mocking his father. However, what he should have done was cover his father's sin and treat him with respect and kindness. In the same way, when another Christian is found in sin, it is our duty as brothers and sisters in Christ to help restore that other believer—not to gloat or gossip about that person's failure. By carefully helping someone who has fallen, we cover that person's shame.

In practical terms, this means that we should lovingly challenge brothers and sisters in Christ who are falling into sinful behavior and urge them to continue walking with God. This must be done discreetly, however, and with much prayer. It should also follow the steps for confrontation and restoration that Jesus laid out in Matthew 18:15–18.

Children are to honor their parents. However Ham's sin is construed, one thing is certain: he did not show honor and respect to his father, Noah. Ham's negative

93

example provided a direct contrast to what God expected of the Israelites, who would have learned about Ham's indiscretion from Moses. Honoring God's authority structure within the family is so important, in fact, that God included it in the Ten Commandments, as the fifth commandment explicitly states: "Honor your father and your mother, that your days may be long upon the land which the Lord your God is giving you" (Exodus 20:12). The irreverence and disrespect that characterized Ham (and, by implication, his descendants through Canaan) was the complete opposite of what God desires of His people.

Our sins may have consequences that affect many more people than just ourselves. Our obedience to God can bring a long-term blessing to others, such as when Noah was obedient in building the ark. However, our disobedience can also bring long-term consequences of sorrow to others, as Ham's indiscretion demonstrated. Because of his sinful actions, he brought a curse on an entire race of people—the Canaanites.

Of course, this is not to say that the Canaanites were not culpable for their own actions. Their sensuality and wickedness mirrored that of their ancestor, Ham. Because of their gross iniquity, they certainly deserved God's judgment (which He brought through the conquering Israelites). Similarly, Adam's sin brought a curse on the entire human race, yet each sinner is personally culpable for his or her own sin before God. The good news is that each sinner can be forgiven from sin and reconciled to God through Jesus Christ.

REFLECTING ON THE TEXT

5) Noah's sin led his son into sin, which affected an entire race of people. What principle does that illustrate about sin? When have you seen evidence of this principle in your own life?

_____

_____

_____

_____

6) In practical terms, what does it mean to "cover" another person's shame?

_____

_____

_____

_____

7) When has someone covered your shame? When has someone exposed it?

_____

_____

_____

_____

8) How does Ham's negative example underscore the importance of the fifth commandment? Why do you think God takes the authority structure within the family so seriously?

_____

_____

_____

_____

PERSONAL RESPONSE

9) How do you generally respond when you learn of another Christian's sin?
Are you more like Ham or more like Shem and Japheth?

_____

_____

_____

_____

10) Children today often fail to honor their parents. What have been the
negative effects of this on our society as it relates to the deterioration of the
family?

_____

_____

_____

_____

10

HERITAGE AND FAMILY
Genesis 10:1–32

DRAWING NEAR

From what country or region did your family originate? What customs and traditions do your family celebrate?

_____

_____

_____

_____

THE CONTEXT

Once again, we find ourselves at the ark. Noah and his family are, as we have noted, the only humans alive on earth, and it is entirely up to them to reestablish the human race. God has given them the same injunction that He gave to Adam at the beginning in the garden of Eden: be fruitful and multiply; fill the earth and subdue it.

As we saw in the last study, modern science has confirmed that all nations and races today had their origins in three distinct "people groups"—descendants of the sons of Noah. Anthropologists and linguists have even surmised that there was originally one common ancestor. Even evolutionists acknowledge that nations and large people groups appeared over a short period of time rather than the billions of years that they use as their safety net for all other ridiculous assertions.

In this study, we will examine what Scripture has to say about the beginnings of the modern human race: where various races and nations came from, how the earth was first populated, and what it means to us today. The account in Genesis 11 of the Tower of Babel (which we will examine in the next study) is actually a zoomed-in detail of the larger matter contained in this chapter: the dispersion of mankind.

TABLE OF THE NATIONS

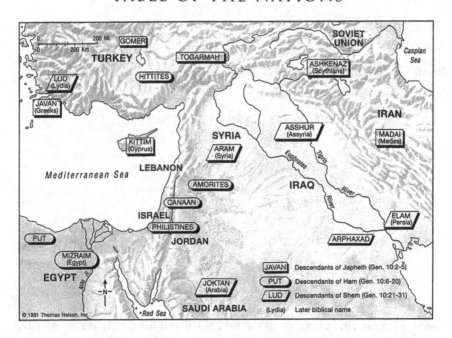

KEYS TO THE TEXT

Read Genesis 10:1–32, noting the key words and phrases indicated below.

> THE DESCENDANTS OF JAPHETH: *Japheth's descendants headed north and west. (Refer to the map in the Introduction for the entire dispersion of the nations.)*

10:2. JAPHETH: The Greeks called themselves Iapetos, which is likely derived from the name Japheth. His descendants settled to the north and west of the Middle East, in what we would today call Asia and Europe.

GOMER: It is theorized that Gomer's descendants moved westward into what we now call Europe. Many people groups still bear a form of his name—the Gauls (French) and the Cymru (Welsh) are probably derivations of the name Gomer.

MAGOG: Probably father of the Scythian peoples. Gog and Magog are used in Scripture to represent the power of the world—and therefore the enemy of God's people (see Ezekiel 38:2; Revelation 20:8).

MADAI: Father of the people known as the Medes, who are prominent in the book of Daniel.

JAVAN: Father of the Greeks. In Daniel 8:21, the name Javan is rendered "Greece" in modern translations. The Greeks were also known as Ionians—a name that is derived directly from Javan.

MESHECH: It is possible that the people of Russia—specifically the Muscovites, who are connected with Moscow—are descended from Meshech.

TIRAS: Possibly the father of the Thracians.

3. TOGARMAH: Possibly the father of the Turks.

4. TARSHISH: The city of Tarsus was named after Tarshish and is best remembered as the birthplace of Paul.

5. GENTILES: The term "Gentiles" may originally have referred specifically to the descendants of Japheth. However, the Bible uses the word generically to refer to any nation other than Israel and metaphorically to refer to the world as opposed to the church.

THE DESCENDANTS OF HAM: Ham's sons headed south, settling in Egypt and Africa.

6. CUSH: Probably father of Arabia, although Cush is also the ancient name for Ethiopia.

MIZRAIM: Father of Egypt.

PUT: Father of Libya.

CANAAN: Father of the Canaanites. The Canaanites are extremely significant in the Israelites' early history; they were the people who occupied the

Promised Land when Joshua led the Israelites in. Noah had pronounced a curse on them in Genesis 9:25, and they were destined to become Israel's greatest enemy during the occupation of the Promised Land.

8. Nimrod: Nimrod in Hebrew means "rebel." He was a powerful leader, a real "man's man." He probably was the one who organized the building of Babel and its tower. He is a picture of the pride of man—a man who glories in his own strength and capabilities, sees what he wants and takes it, and feels he has no need for God. The kingdoms that Nimrod founded include several that proved to be deadly enemies of God's people.

10. Babel: We will examine the city of Babel and its infamous tower in the next study. Babel is probably the original city of Babylon, which looms large in Scripture as the archetype of man's prideful folly (see also Revelation 17–18).

Erech: This might be the modern nation of Iraq, where the ancient city of Babylon still exists. Iraq has been no friend of Israel in modern times.

Accad: The common language spoken in Mesopotamia was Accadian.

Land of Shinar: Probably Mesopotamia. It appears that the four kingdoms of Babel, Erech, Accad, and Calneh were united together under one strong leader. If so, this is the first appearance of a "United Nations" on earth, and Nimrod figures as a precursor to the Antichrist.

11. Assyria: This was Israel's primary enemy from the east. This powerful nation plagued Israel for many generations.

Nineveh: This is the city to which Jonah would one day travel—reluctantly.

14. Philistines: These people would plague Israel for hundreds of years until finally put down by King David.

16–18. the Jebusite ... Hamathite: Moses switched here from naming specific people and the cities that they founded to naming nations. Many of these nations, such as the Jebusites and Amorites, would become the enemies of Israel as the Jews moved into the Promised Land.

19. border of the Canaanites: This territory includes most of the Promised Land. A region known as the Gaza Strip still exists today—it is infamous as the site even now of bloody struggle against the Jews. Sodom and Gomorrah would one day become prominent in the life of Abraham, and Sodom is notorious for adding a word to the English language: "sodomy."

THE DESCENDANTS OF SHEM: Shem's descendants settled in what we now call the Middle East. Shem is the ancestor of Abraham as well as of Jesus.

21. SHEM: Shem is the father of all races that are named after him, which are called the Semitic people. This includes Israel as well as many others.

THE BROTHER OF JAPHETH THE ELDER: Remember that the actual birth order of Noah's three sons is disputed, and different Bible translations render this verse in different ways. As previously discussed, Shem is the son through whom Jesus would enter the world—the highest honor and "birthright" that could ever be given to a person. A birthright was ordinarily given to the first-born, which argues that Shem was oldest. However, in Genesis almost all the birthrights in the Messiah's line were given to someone other than the oldest, which suggests that Shem might have been the middle son.

EBER: Eber is an ancestor of Abraham. His name led to the word "Hebrew," which was first used to describe Abraham.

30. MESHA: The ancient name for Mecca. Modern-day Arabs are also descended from Shem. The enemies of Israel came as much through Shem as through his brothers.

UNLEASHING THE TEXT

1) From which of Noah's sons are you descended? How far back can you trace your family history?

_____

_____

_____

_____

_____

2) What do the names found in Genesis 10 tell you about how mankind has
   spread out after the Flood?

_____

_____

_____

_____

_____

3) In what ways does this chapter foreshadow events to come in the Bible?
   Events that are still occurring today? Events that are yet to come?

_____

_____

_____

_____

_____

4) How many of the nations and peoples mentioned in this passage became
   enemies of Israel? What principle does this suggest concerning God's
   people in the world today?

_____

_____

_____

_____

EXPLORING THE MEANING

The line of Shem was the line of the promised Deliverer, who would bring salvation to the whole world. It is worth noting that this genealogy lists numerous nations that would turn against Israel in the coming generations. The lesson here is that there is only one chosen people, descended through Shem alone, down through Abraham and David, and culminating in the person of Jesus Christ. The enemies of God's people, however, are descended through all three sons of Noah.

In Christ, the people of God are no longer made up of just ethnic Jews. The church consists of those from all nations and language groups (including those nations that were historically enemies of Israel), because the gospel transcends cultures and borders. Yet just like the saints of the Old Testament, those who belong to Jesus Christ can expect to receive persecution from the unbelieving world.

Mankind did not evolve; we are all descended from Noah. Once again, we find that Genesis rejects the modern notions of evolution—which, in fact, are not modern at all, but ancient. Evolution teaches that mankind slowly grew out of the lower orders of creation and that he gradually developed the skills needed to thrive in civilized communities. Yet even evolutionists are forced to confess the truth of what we read in Genesis 10—that those civilized communities appeared on earth suddenly and all began in the area we call the Middle East.

The Bible answered this question thousands of years ago when Moses wrote his history of the human race. He focused deliberately on the line of Shem because he was teaching the Israelites about their personal family history. The Holy Spirit guided Moses to write these things, because He knew what Moses did not know: that the Messiah would eventually arrive on earth through that genealogical line.

If we refuse to believe that Moses' accounts are true and accurate in the book of Genesis, we imperil our very belief in the person and work of Jesus Christ.

God is always at work fulfilling His promises. When God makes a promise, it is absolutely and completely certain that He will fulfill it. However, this may take a long time—from man's perspective, at least.

God promised Adam and Eve in the garden of Eden that He would send a Deliverer to release mankind from the curse of sin and death. From that moment on, He began to unfold His plan for man's salvation. Even when He was forced by man's sinfulness to destroy the earth, He still preserved a remnant through whom He would keep His word.

In this chapter in Genesis, we see another step in that fulfillment, as God deliberately separates His chosen people from the rest of the world. It has taken a long time in human terms to reach this point—probably around 1,800 years—and it will be a longer time still before Jesus Himself appears to fulfill the promise. But God has been working faithfully the entire time.

REFLECTING ON THE TEXT

5) What have you been taught regarding the history of the human race?

_____

_____

_____

_____

_____

6) How does Genesis 10 compare with what the world says? Which do you
believe? Why?

_____

_____

_____

_____

_____

7) If Shem was, in fact, not the firstborn, then he had no natural right to expect such a blessing. What does this demonstrate about the men and women God uses?

_____

_____

_____

_____

8) Why did God select Shem as a forbearer of Christ? Why not Japheth or Ham?

_____

_____

_____

_____

PERSONAL RESPONSE

9) What promises do you feel God has been "slow" in keeping to you? In what ways have you been startled to see His hand at work in your life?

_____

_____

_____

_____

10) What benefits have you found in being a member of the family of God? If you are not yet a member, what is preventing you from making that step?

_____

_____

_____

_____

11

THE TOWER OF BABEL
Genesis 11:1–8

DRAWING NEAR

How has modern science or technology affected your life in good ways? In bad ways?

_____

_____

_____

_____

THE CONTEXT

The years have rolled forward, and Noah and his family have now settled into their home in the "new earth" after the Flood. They begin to repopulate the planet as God has instructed. Over time, the descendants of Noah begin to build towns and villages and cities.

At this point in history, all mankind speaks one language—probably the language that Adam spoke with God in the garden of Eden. Having one common language made it possible for mankind to unite together in carrying out great projects. In this chapter in Genesis, we will see how they would use that gift: to build a great city that would bring glory to themselves.

God looks down and sees that mankind has not changed since the Flood. Man is still intent on becoming a god unto himself, excluding the lordship of his Creator. This time, however, the Lord does not send a great flood to destroy mankind from the face of the earth. Instead, He confuses man's language, making it difficult for humanity to join together in an effort to become "like God." This confusion of languages will also lead to the dispersion of mankind throughout the planet—which is what God had commanded man to do in the first place.

KEYS TO THE TEXT

Read Genesis 11:1–8, noting the key words and phrases indicated below.

> ONE LIP: *The entire human race shares one language, which enables men to unite together for great projects.*

11:1. WHOLE EARTH: This most likely means roughly the area that we would now refer to as the Middle East. At this point, the descendants of Noah—who constitute the whole human race—have not spread throughout the planet. God had commanded Noah, "Be fruitful and multiply, and fill the earth" (Genesis 9:1), but his descendants had apparently disregarded this injunction. Filling the earth would have required that men separate and strike out on their own—a prospect that involved risk. It was far easier to band together and build cities, enabling men to rely on themselves and one another rather than stepping out with faith in God.

ONE LANGUAGE AND ONE SPEECH: Literally, "one lip and one word." This phrase emphasizes with its repetition that all human beings spoke the same language and had the same vocabulary—they used the same words and phrases. Modern Americans, for example, speak the same language as modern British people, yet the two cultures differ in vocabulary and turns of phrase. Such differences even exist within cultures; one can find distinct differences of dialect as one travels throughout the United States. But such differences evidently did not exist at all in man's early history. This unity of speech made communication easy and enabled mankind to unite and work together cooperatively. Also, it is important to remember that man alone had the gift of speech—a gift that God had given to Adam specifically so that he could communicate with Him and other people. In this chapter in Genesis, we discover that mankind has always corrupted God's gifts for his own pleasures.

2. AS THEY JOURNEYED FROM THE EAST: Many translations render this, "as they journeyed eastward." If the Mount Ararat where the ark landed is the same Ararat that we know of in modern Turkey, then it seems likely that Noah's descendants moved *toward* the east—provided, of course, that the Tower of Babel was built in Babylon, which is located in modern-day Iraq. Obviously, we cannot be entirely certain of the exact locations of these sites.

SHINAR: Probably Mesopotamia.

THE GREAT PROJECT: *We will now watch and see what mankind will do with his gift of unity and communication. God, as it turns out, is also watching.*

3. THEY SAID TO ONE ANOTHER: This is the first subtle hint that men were turning to themselves rather than to God. There is nothing wrong with people uniting together to create things—indeed, this is part of what it means to be made in God's image. It quickly becomes apparent, however, that man was still trying to become his own god rather than submitting himself before his Creator.

LET US MAKE BRICKS: Here we see mankind acting in the image of God, creating things that didn't exist before (although man is limited to creating from existing materials, while God can create something out of nothing). This is an early example of people coming together to invent new technologies.

THEY HAD BRICK FOR STONE: Here we see mankind also uniting to overcome environmental obstacles. There apparently was not any stone in the region that was suitable for construction, but this shortage did not stop man from accomplishing his goal.

GLORY TO MAN: *The true nature of man's heart is now revealed: he is seeking his own glory. Man is trying once again to worship himself rather than his Creator.*

4. LET US BUILD OURSELVES: Here we discover a problem: mankind's focus was on itself, not on God. By making this statement, the people were revealing the true motivation of their building schemes.

A CITY: Archeologists believe that this city was the early foundation for what would become Babylon. The city of Babylon is important in Scripture, as it represents the worldly enemy of the people of God.

A TOWER: This may have been a ziggurat, a large structure composed of concentric squares rising to a great height. Such structures were fairly common in the Babylonian region and were generally used as temples to pagan gods.

WHOSE TOP IS IN THE HEAVENS: This was actually an ancient form of humanistic thinking: that mankind could raise itself to become equal with God. In Genesis 3 we saw where this lie originated, yet man still thinks this way in modern times.

LET US MAKE A NAME FOR OURSELVES: Man's underlying goal is again revealed: bringing glory to himself and his achievements. There is no mention of God—whether seeking His will, bringing glory to His name, or even obeying His commands.

LEST WE BE SCATTERED ABROAD: This was man's one reference to God's commands—and it was a determination *not* to obey them. Man was determined not to obey God's instructions to spread out and populate the entire earth, so God would have to force man to obey. It is worth noting that man appeared to be *afraid* of spreading out across the earth. There is an interesting paradox here: mankind's motives were a combination of pride, hoping to bring glory to itself, and fear—fear of being "scattered abroad." To be "scattered" is to be forced to move abroad, whereas God had commanded them to "fill the earth"—something that would have been done voluntarily. Man simply could not accept the concept of God telling him what to do. He wanted to be his own god.

GOD INVESTIGATES: *The Lord Himself descends to earth—not to bring judgment, but to seek for a way of extending grace.*

5. THE LORD CAME DOWN TO SEE: In Genesis, God generally came down to earth in physical form to bring judgment. However, His motivation in such "reconnaissance missions" was always to seek an opportunity to extend grace. Here we find Him coming to the earth to investigate the great city and tower that mankind was building, and it is likely He was doing so to see if He could defer His judgment.

6. THE PEOPLE ARE ONE: Here we discover an interesting insight that goes directly against the universal thinking of modern mankind: it is not good for fallen humanity to be united as one! God declared that it was dangerous for sinful mankind to be so united. It was, in fact, an act of divine mercy when He frustrated men's language and scattered them abroad.

NOTHING THAT THEY PROPOSE TO DO WILL BE WITHHELD FROM THEM: The implication of this statement is that if God were to withhold His hand, man would go from bad to worse. His observation that "this is what they begin to do" suggests that the human race was heading back toward the level of depravity they had reached during the days of Noah when God was forced to slay all the living. If God did not intervene quickly, the entire human race would slip back into the deepest levels of wickedness.

GOD'S MERCIFUL JUDGMENT: The Lord pronounces His judgment and scatters mankind abroad for its own protection.

7. LET US: God is speaking to Himself, just as He did when He decided to create mankind in the first place (see Genesis 1:26).

CONFUSE THEIR LANGUAGE: Again, as we have discussed, God was actually being merciful at this point, because the united civilization was heading rapidly toward major disaster. By making it difficult to communicate together, God effectively forced men to divide themselves into independent cities and nations. It is interesting how hard we have strived to overcome this barrier today. We are in an age of increasing worldwide communications, and the Internet, satellite communications, smartphones, and other technologies are coming together to close the language gap. On the surface this seems like a good thing, but the book of Revelation reveals that the global reunification of mankind will ultimately end in disaster.

8. THE LORD SCATTERED THEM ABROAD: Man's worst fears were realized. Ironically, this scattering did not bring destruction to mankind; on the contrary, it led to man's dominion over the entire planet. Although men may refuse to obey God, they will ultimately be forced into compliance. God's will shall be done, whether man wills it or not. In the end, "every knee shall bow . . . and every tongue shall confess" (Romans 14:11)—voluntarily or otherwise—that Jesus Christ is Lord.

9. BABEL: A play on a Hebrew word meaning "confusion." Again, the location is uncertain, but it is probably the ancient city of Babylon, located in modern-day Iraq.

UNLEASHING THE TEXT

1) What exactly was mankind doing in this passage that was displeasing to God? Why were they doing these things? Why was God not pleased?

_____

_____

_____

_____

_____

2) Why did God want people to spread out and populate the earth?

_____

_____

_____

_____

_____

3) Why do you think the descendants of Noah failed to follow this command?

_____

_____

_____

_____

4) When have you experienced the frustration of poor communication? When has a misunderstanding worked out for good in your life?

_____

_____

_____

_____

EXPLORING THE MEANING

Man's greatest achievements cannot remove the curse. From the beginning of human history, people have tried to elevate themselves above the constraints of earth and, ultimately, above the curse of death. It was Adam's desire to elevate himself to the level of God that brought the curse on mankind in the first place. We see the same behavior repeated at the Tower of Babel.

Mankind has not changed over time, and we are still pursuing the same futile dream in the twenty-first century. We are driven by the hope that modern science, medicine, technology, and other fields of study will enable us to one day evolve into a higher plane of existence beyond the threat of disease and death. Even our present-day space exploration represents an attempt by people of different nations to cooperate, communicate, and work together— again in the hopes of escaping the confines of their earthly environment.

However, the Bible is clear: wherever man goes, he carries the curse of sin along with him. There will never be any escape from death until God Himself sets up His eternal kingdom (see Revelation 21:1–4).

Man's natural instinct is to abuse God's gifts. We saw this principle at work right at the beginning, when Adam abused his privileged status by choosing to disobey rather than to obey. We see it again in Genesis 11, when mankind used the gifts of speech and creativity to bring glory to self rather than to God.

This is the natural tendency of man: to elevate self to equality with God in an effort to avoid being accountable to the Creator. The end result is always the same: man is alienated from his fellow men and also from God. The good news, however, is that this is *not* the natural tendency of *regenerate* man. We are given freedom from the bondage of our sinful nature through the Holy Spirit, who enters our lives when we accept God's gift of rebirth through the blood of Christ. Through Jesus, we gain a new set of gifts—spiritual gifts—and learn a new way of using those gifts to the glory of God.

God is always working to offer grace. God often descended to earth in the book of Genesis because the sin of mankind had reached a point of crisis. He came down to investigate and see whether the reports of man's wickedness were true. This was not because He lacked knowledge—because He didn't know for sure—but because He was looking for a way of offering grace to sinful human beings.

We saw this in the garden of Eden, when God came to Adam and led him to confession of sin (see Genesis 3). God confronted Cain and offered him guidance on how to repent and avoid greater sins (see Genesis 4). He would later come to Abraham to seek a way of avoiding the destruction of Sodom and Gomorrah (see Genesis 18). And He came to the Tower of Babel, looking for a way to prevent mankind from completing their reckless path toward destruction.

Ultimately, God would come to earth in human form in the person of Jesus Christ. This would be the ultimate act of grace and redemption, bought at the ultimate price: His own death on the cross. Yet this also shows us how much God desires to be reconciled with mankind.

REFLECTING ON THE TEXT

5) In what ways are modern societies repeating the mistakes of the people at Babel?

_____

_____

_____

_____

6) When have you relied on other people, or on technology or science, rather than on God? When have you been forced to rely on God alone?

_____

_____

_____

_____

_____

7) When have you tried to avoid obeying God's Word? What was the result?

_____

_____

_____

_____

_____

8) How have you seen God's grace in your own life?

_____

_____

_____

_____

_____

PERSONAL RESPONSE

9) Are you using the gifts of God for your own profit or for His glory? Is your life characterized more by your own glory or the glory of God?

_____

_____

_____

_____

10) In what area is God asking you to be more obedient to Him?

_____

_____

_____

_____

12

REVIEWING KEY PRINCIPLES

DRAWING NEAR

As you look back at each of the studies in Genesis 1–11, what is the one thing that stood out to you the most? What is one new perspective you have learned?

_____

_____

_____

_____

THE CONTEXT

We have covered a significant period of human history during these studies, beginning at day 1 of creation and progressing to the year 2150 BC or thereabouts—roughly 2,000 years. The most significant and momentous events in human history—apart from the work of Christ—have occurred during this time.

The way that we understand and treat the early chapters of Genesis will determine how we treat the rest of the Bible. Our view of creation and sin and redemption will color our view of Jesus Himself. These issues are of immense importance to Christians, and we must take care that we truly understand what Moses was teaching in these chapters.

The following represents a few of the major themes that we have discussed. There are many others that are not included here, so take time to review the earlier studies—or, better still, to meditate on the passages in Scripture that we have covered. Ask that the Holy Spirit would give you wisdom and insight into His Word.

EXPLORING THE MEANING

God is always at work to bring His grace to mankind. Genesis 1–11 records numerous instances in which mankind had done something so bad that the human race was subject to God's wrath. Yet in each of these instances (such as the Fall, Cain's murder, the Flood, and the Tower of Babel), God extended His grace. God is eager to show forth His grace and slow to unleash His wrath.

We also should remember that His plan sometimes takes a long time—at least from a human perspective. He promised Adam and Eve that He would send them a Redeemer to lift the curse of death, yet it was some 4,000 years before Christ was even born. The final fulfillment of that promise is still in the future, when Christ will set up His eternal kingdom and abolish the curse of death forever.

God's patience with sinful man is, in fact, the reason why He has not already established Christ's future kingdom. There are still more people whom He desires to graciously save.

Man was created directly by God, in His image, in one 24-hour day. We have seen this theme throughout the first 11 chapters of Genesis, beginning at creation and continuing through the dispersion of the human race into what even evolutionists confess to be the early civilizations of mankind. God's Word simply will not tolerate any element of evolutionary teaching. It is abundantly clear, right from the beginning, that God created the universe in six literal days. No element of evolution enters into it.

This particular principle is contentious in the church today, as a great many teachers and theologians have claimed that the word "day" in Genesis 1 actually means "a great period of time." However, as we have seen in our studies, God's Word reiterates the fact that God simply spoke and all life—human and otherwise—came into existence, literally and fully completed.

The long-term danger of trying to force evolution into Genesis is that we negate the Bible's teachings on sin and man's need for a Redeemer, which, in turn, devalues the work of Christ. The New Testament is perfectly clear on this matter: death entered the world through the literal sin of one literal man named Adam, and death did not exist in the world prior to his sin. If there was no death, and hence no natural selection, there was no evolution.

God ordained an order at the time of creation—a hierarchy of authority. God created the human race to rule over the rest of creation and be in headship of it. Adam was created first, and Eve from his rib, because Adam was created to be in headship over his wife and their descendants. Satan entered the garden of Eden with the intention of turning this created order upside down. He wanted to tempt Adam and Eve to commit an act of rebellion against God's authority.

Today, this issue of headship is still a touchy topic in the world—and in the church. The reason why it is so controversial is that it is important. It is important to God's people, and to God's church, that we observe and submit to His created order. This has implications concerning the roles of women and men within the church and the home, the respect of children toward their parents, and the proper attitude of submission people should have to worldly authorities.

The concept of headship goes all the way back to the week of creation—before sin and death entered the world. Authority structure is woven into the very fabric of creation, and mankind ignores or supplants it with disastrous results.

God's Word does not require some "higher knowledge" for clear understanding. Many people within the church today claim that we cannot fully understand the early chapters of Genesis without first gaining some extra knowledge—knowledge of modern science or anthropology or archeology or ancient pagan texts. This is a false claim.

God's Word is His written revelation of Himself to mankind, and as such God intends that it be clear and understandable to all who read it. This does not mean that there are not passages that will make a person stop and ponder—quite the opposite, in fact. God's Word will frequently go directly against the teachings of the world, and it may even become a "stumbling block" to those who read it. This stumbling occurs when people are forced to choose between the teachings of men and the Word of God.

Knowledge itself is a good thing. Indeed, it is the very purpose of the Bible that men and women may come to know God. Some advanced learning can even be a useful tool in this process—the ability to read Greek or Hebrew, for example, is helpful in gaining insight into the meaning of the original manuscripts. However, these things are *not* required to understand what the Scriptures mean. The only things necessary are a regenerate heart, a willing attitude (to submit to what the Bible plainly teaches), and the Holy Spirit's guidance.

God is both merciful and just. God extends His mercy and grace to all men, having made known to the world the gospel of grace—that salvation from sin and death can be found through His Son, Jesus Christ. However, God's justice must also be satisfied. Those who accept Christ as their Savior have already satisfied God's justice through the sacrifice of Jesus. Those who reject that gift, however, will discover that they have an eternal debt to pay. Either way, God's justice will be satisfied.

Sadly, those who attempt to pay their own debt to God—or deny that they even *have* any debt to God—will also discover that they cannot pay the debt. God's justice demands a blood sacrifice for sin, not a works sacrifice or a "nice person" sacrifice. Noah's neighbors had ample time to repent of their sins and turn to God for salvation, but the day finally came when God's justice rained down on them. They had made their own decisions, and they found themselves facing the justice of God.

God's people are called to cover sin, not to gloat. God's people should work diligently and mercifully to help erring brothers and sisters. We should love them and cover their shame rather than take pleasure in discovering it.

The words of James summarize this concept: "Brethren, if anyone among you wanders from the truth, and someone turns him back, let him know that he who turns a sinner from the error of his way will save a soul from death and cover a multitude of sins" (James 5:19–20). Peter reminds us that "love will cover a multitude of sins" (1 Peter 4:8; see also Proverbs 10:12).

In practical terms, this means that we should lovingly challenge brothers and sisters in Christ who are falling into sinful behavior and urge them to continue walking with God. We should do this discreetly, according to the process that Jesus articulated in Matthew 18, and with much prayer. It never includes gloating or gossip.

We are called to walk with God. Noah is only one of many in Scripture who "walked with God." These were men and women whose lives were characterized by a consciousness of God's presence at all times. Everywhere they went, they walked as though God were beside them. Every word they spoke and every action of their lives was marked with the recognition that God was watching and listening. This lifestyle is attainable by all who have accepted Jesus as Savior, because we have the Holy Spirit dwelling within us—and He desires this lifestyle for us even more than we do ourselves!

The key was demonstrated by Noah: trust and obey. Noah was quick to worship God, quick to believe His word, and quick to obey. This is still the way to walk with God in our century.

UNLEASHING THE TEXT

1) Which of the concepts or principles in the first 11 chapters of Genesis have you found to be the most encouraging? Why?

_____

_____

_____

_____

2) Which of the concepts or principles have you found most challenging? Why?

_____

_____

_____

_____

3) What aspects of "walking with God" are you already doing in your life? Which areas need strengthening?

_____

_____

_____

4) To which of the characters that we've studied have you most been able to relate? How might you emulate that person in your own life?

_____

_____

_____

PERSONAL RESPONSE

5) Have you taken a definite stand for Jesus Christ? Have you accepted His free gift of salvation? If not, what is preventing you?

_____

_____

_____

_____

6) In which areas of your life have you been the most convicted during this study? What exact things will you do to address these convictions? Be specific.

_____

_____

_____

_____

7) What have you learned about the character of God during this study? How has this insight affected your worship or prayer life?

_____

_____

_____

_____

8) What are some specific things that you want to see God do in your life during the coming month? What are some things that you intend to change in your own life during that time? (Return to this list in one month and hold yourself accountable to fulfill these things.)

_____

_____

_____

_____

If you would like to continue in your study of the Old Testament, read the next title in this series: _Genesis 12–33: The Father of Israel._

ALSO AVAILABLE

In this study, John MacArthur guides readers through an in-depth look at the historical period beginning with Abraham's call from God, continuing through his relocation in the land of Canaan, and concluding with the story of his grandsons Jacob and Esau. This study includes close-up examinations of Sarah, Hagar, Ishmael, and Isaac, as well as careful considerations of doctrinal themes such as "Covenant and Obedience" and "Wrestling with God."

The MacArthur Bible Studies provide intriguing examinations of the whole of Scripture. Each guide incorporates extensive commentary, detailed observations on overriding themes, and probing questions to help you study the Word of God with guidance from John MacArthur.

9780718033743-B

ALSO AVAILABLE

JOHN MACARTHUR

GENESIS
34–50

JACOB AND EGYPT

MacArthur Bible Studies

In this study, John MacArthur guides readers through an in-depth look at the historical period beginning with Jacob's first encounter with Rachel, continuing through their son Joseph's captivity as an Egyptian slave, and concluding with the dramatic rescue of Jacob's family. This study includes close-up examinations of Dinah (Jacob's daughter), Judah, Tamar, and Pharaoh's chief butler, as well as careful considerations of doctrinal themes such as "The Sovereignty of God" and "Finishing in Faith."

The MacArthur Bible Studies provide intriguing examinations of the whole of Scripture. Each guide incorporates extensive commentary, detailed observations on overriding themes, and probing questions to help you study the Word of God with guidance from John MacArthur.

9780718033743-B

ALSO AVAILABLE

I n this study, John MacArthur guides readers through an in-depth look at the historical period beginning with God's calling of Moses, continuing through the giving of the Ten Commandments, and concluding with the Israelites' preparations to enter the Promised Land. This study includes close-up examinations of Aaron, Caleb, Joshua, Balaam and Balak, as well as careful considerations of doctrinal themes such as "Complaints and Rebellion" and "Following God's Law."

The MacArthur Bible Studies provide intriguing examinations of the whole of Scripture. Each guide incorporates extensive commentary, detailed observations on overriding themes, and probing questions to help you study the Word of God with guidance from John MacArthur.

9780718033743-C